Foreword

Welcome, fellow travelers on the green and digital paths, to a journey unlike any you've embarked on before. This book isn't just another tome on the complexities of financial markets or a dry, technical manual on cryptocurrency trading. No, friends, it's a guide designed for you, the stoner with a keen eye on the future and a joint in hand, looking to navigate the tumultuous waters of Bitcoin day trading.

In these pages, you'll find a sanctuary where the worlds of high finance and high times collide. We'll explore the ethereal realm of Bitcoin - a digital currency that has shaken the foundations of traditional banking with its promise of decentralization, anonymity, and a new form of wealth generation. For those of you who've spent more time pondering the mysteries of the universe than pondering over financial statements, fear not. We're here to break down what Bitcoin is, how it works, and why it's captured the imagination of millions worldwide, all in a language that feels like a conversation with an old friend.

Day trading, the art of buying and selling assets within a single trading day, can seem like a high-stakes game reserved for the Wall Street elite. Yet, we'll show you that with the right mindset, tools, and a bit of wisdom passed down from traders of yore, you too can partake in this digital gold rush without losing your shirt or your chill.

This book is structured to walk you through every step of your day trading journey. From setting up your digital wallet (think of it as your stash box for Bitcoin) to crafting a trading plan that aligns with your lifestyle and risk tolerance (because even in trading, it's all about balance), we've got you covered. We'll delve into market analysis with a twist, offering insights into charts and patterns without making your head spin. And when it comes to executing trades, we'll share strategies on when to make your move and how to do so with confidence, even when the market's as volatile as a debate on indica vs. sativa.

Beyond the nuts and bolts of trading, this book is also about embracing the day trader lifestyle while staying true to your laid-back roots. It's possible to be both a successful trader and a staunch member of the stoner community, and we'll show you how to blend these aspects of your identity seamlessly. From managing stress and avoiding common pitfalls to diversifying your portfolio like a well-curated munchies spread, we'll provide you with the tools and knowledge to grow not just as a trader, but as a person.

So, light up, sit back, and let's embark on this journey together. Whether you're here to turn a profit, to understand the world of Bitcoin, or simply for the love of the adventure, you're in good company. Welcome to the high life of day trading Bitcoin.

Chapter 1

The Highs and Lows of Bitcoin

In the sprawling digital landscape, where innovation blooms like the rarest of strains in a cultivator's garden, there exists a commodity as sought after as the most elusive bud – cryptocurrency. Imagine wandering into your local dispensary with a desire to experience something groundbreaking, only to find out there's a strain so unique, so revolutionary, that it's not just grown in a hidden corner of the world but also exists solely in a digital realm. That, my friends, is the essence of cryptocurrency.

Cryptocurrency, at its core, is digital money. But not the kind that's tied to any country or bank. No, this is something entirely different. It's decentralized, meaning it's not controlled by any single entity. Instead, it thrives in a sprawling network of computers, each working to secure and verify transactions in a way that's transparent yet anonymous. Think of it as a communal grow operation for a super strain, where everyone involved cares for the crop, yet no one claims sole ownership. The harvest? A secure, digital token that can be exchanged as easily as passing a joint at a party.

The beauty of cryptocurrency lies in its decentralization. Traditional money systems are like a tightly controlled grow house, where access is restricted, and every move is monitored. Cryptocurrencies, however, grow in the wild expanse of the digital world, nurtured by a community that values freedom, privacy, and innovation. This open environment ensures that no single person can dictate the flow or distribution of this digital currency, making it a truly democratic form of money.

The star of this digital currency revolution is, without a doubt, Bitcoin. It's the OG strain of the cryptocurrency world – the one that started it all. Launched in the depths of the internet in 2009 by the mysterious Satoshi Nakamoto, Bitcoin introduced us to the concept of blockchain technology – a decentralized ledger that records every transaction. Picture a grow journal that's not kept under lock and key but is instead posted on the wall for everyone to see, verify, and trust. That's the blockchain, ensuring that every exchange of Bitcoin is as transparent as it is secure, without needing a middleman to validate it.

So, why is Bitcoin, and cryptocurrency in general, as desirable as that legendary strain everyone talks about but few have tasted? It's because it represents freedom – the freedom to transact without oversight, the freedom from the whims of banks and governments, and the freedom to be part of a financial revolution from anywhere, at any time. Like discovering a new way to enjoy cannabis that elevates the experience to unprecedented heights, Bitcoin offers a new way to think about and use money, untethered by the constraints of traditional financial systems.

As we delve deeper into the world of Bitcoin and cryptocurrency, keep this analogy in mind. It's about more than just digital transactions; it's about participating in a global movement that's as liberating as it is thrilling. Welcome to the future of finance, where the digital and the decentralized bloom together in a vibrant ecosystem of innovation and freedom.

In the annals of digital revolution, there exists a genesis story that rivals the tales of underground movements and counterculture icons. This is the story of Bitcoin's birth, a tale not of a person, place, or thing, but of an idea powerful enough to start a financial revolution. At the heart of this narrative is a figure shrouded in mystery, known only by the pseudonym Satoshi Nakamoto. Like the elusive creator of a legendary cannabis strain that changes the game, Satoshi Nakamoto's true identity remains a mystery, adding a layer of intrigue to Bitcoin's origins.

In 2008, as the world reeled from financial turmoil and a crisis of trust in banking institutions, a paper titled "Bitcoin: A Peer-to-Peer Electronic Cash System" was quietly published on a cryptography mailing list. This whitepaper, authored by Nakamoto, proposed a radical new concept: a digital currency that could operate independently of central banks, using a decentralized network to verify transactions. Picture the moment a groundbreaking album drops, its new sound destined to influence generations. Satoshi's whitepaper was the financial equivalent, promising to upend the way we thought about money.

The core innovation introduced by Bitcoin was the blockchain, a digital ledger where transactions are recorded chronologically and publicly. Think of it as the ultimate tracklist of financial exchanges, each song (transaction) contributing to an album (blockchain) that tells the story of Bitcoin's journey. This decentralized approach ensured that no single institution could control or manipulate the currency, a direct response to the centralized control blamed for the financial crash.

Satoshi's vision was more than just a technical solution; it was a call to arms, echoing the rebellious spirit of the 60s and 70s counterculture movements. Just as those movements sought to challenge the status quo and inspire change, Bitcoin aimed to disrupt the established financial order and democratize access to wealth. It wasn't just about creating a new type of currency; it was about challenging the very foundation of financial sovereignty and offering an alternative path forward.

Mining the first block of Bitcoin, known as the Genesis Block, in January 2009, Satoshi kickstarted what would become a global phenomenon. The message embedded in this first block, "The Times 03/Jan/2009 Chancellor on brink of second bailout for banks," served as a poignant reminder of Bitcoin's anti-establishment roots, much like a protest song that captures the mood of a generation.

Satoshi's involvement with Bitcoin was like a fleeting visitation; after laying the groundwork and shepherding the early community, they faded into the background, leaving a legacy that would grow beyond anyone's wildest imaginations. Their departure was akin to the mythical figures of folklore who leave behind treasures with the potential to change the world.

The birth of Bitcoin marked the beginning of a new era in finance, one where freedom, privacy, and decentralization were not just ideals but realities. As we explore the impact and evolution of this digital currency, remember that, at its core, Bitcoin is more than a technological marvel; it's the embodiment of a revolution, a dream of a world where financial power is returned to the people, much like the aspirations that fueled the counterculture movements of the past.

Imagine you're part of a tight-knit community of growers, each cultivating their own unique strains. To ensure transparency and trust, you all decide to keep a communal grow journal. In this journal, every entry details who's growing what, the progress of each plant, and every exchange of seeds and buds. This journal is kept in a secure location where everyone has access, but no single person can alter its entries without everyone else knowing. This system ensures that every contribution is recorded, every transaction is clear, and trust is maintained within the community. This, in essence, is what blockchain technology is all about.

Blockchain is the digital equivalent of this communal grow journal. It's a public ledger, but instead of tracking strains of cannabis, it records transactions of digital currency, like Bitcoin. Each transaction is a "block" of data, which includes information about the sender, receiver, and the amount transferred. Once a transaction is verified by the network through a process called mining, it's added to the "chain" of previous transactions. This chain forms a complete, unalterable history of all transactions made with that cryptocurrency.

Think of each block as an individual plant in our communal garden. Just as a plant starts from a seed and grows over time, each block starts with a single transaction and becomes part of a larger, interconnected structure. And just like how each plant's growth is visible to the entire community, each block added to the blockchain is visible to anyone who wants to see it, ensuring transparency and security.

The decentralized nature of blockchain is like having multiple copies of our grow journal spread throughout the community. If someone tried to change an entry in one copy, it wouldn't match the others, and the discrepancy would be immediately obvious. This makes the blockchain incredibly secure; to alter a transaction, someone would need to change the block containing that transaction and all subsequent blocks in every copy of the ledger simultaneously, a task so computationally demanding as to be virtually impossible.

Moreover, just as our communal journal fosters trust and collaboration by openly sharing the journey of each strain from seed to harvest, blockchain technology fosters trust among its users. It enables people to make transactions directly with each other, without needing a trusted third party like a bank or government to verify those transactions. This not only makes transactions quicker and cheaper but also returns control of money to the people, embodying the decentralized, democratic ethos at the heart of cryptocurrency.

In sum, blockchain is the foundation upon which the entire cryptocurrency world is built. It's what makes digital currencies like Bitcoin not just a new form of money, but a new way of thinking about what money is and what it can do. Just as our hypothetical communal garden would revolutionize how we think about growing and sharing, blockchain technology has the potential to transform how we think about and use money in a digital age.

Diving deeper into the world of Bitcoin, let's explore the concepts of mining and transactions, using familiar analogies to bring these technical processes to life. Think of Bitcoin mining as the digital equivalent of searching for rare vinyl records. Just as crate-digging DJs scour record stores, flea markets, and garage sales for that elusive vinyl to complete their collection, Bitcoin miners use their computers to solve complex mathematical puzzles. The reward for discovering a new block (akin to finding that rare record) is a set of newly minted Bitcoins — the blockchain's way of saying, "Congratulations, you've added something valuable to the community."

Mining is the heartbeat of the Bitcoin ecosystem. It's not just about creating new coins; it's also how transactions are verified and added to the blockchain. When a miner successfully solves a puzzle and adds a block to the chain, that block contains a record of several transactions. This process is crucial because it ensures the integrity and security of the decentralized ledger without the need for a central authority. Imagine throwing a massive block party where everyone's invited, and you find that rare record to play. The joy isn't just in the finding; it's in sharing that music with everyone, enhancing the party's vibe. Mining shares this communal spirit by validating transactions and spreading the wealth of new coins.

Now, let's talk about transactions. Picture this: you've got a rare mixtape that your friend has been dying to listen to, and they have a concert poster you've been wanting to add to your collection. You decide to swap — the mixtape for the poster. In the world of Bitcoin, transactions work similarly. If you want to send Bitcoin to someone, you're essentially transferring ownership of a digital asset from one digital wallet to another. This transaction is broadcast to the Bitcoin network, where miners pick it up and add it to a block of transactions. Once the block is mined, and the transaction is verified, the transfer is complete. The digital "mixtape" has been swapped, no middleman required.

What makes these transactions particularly special in the Bitcoin world is their security and transparency. Each transaction is encrypted and recorded on the blockchain, visible to anyone who wants to see it. This doesn't mean your personal details are out there for everyone to see; your identity is protected by cryptographic keys, ensuring privacy. It's like knowing exactly where the mixtape has traveled through the party, without knowing the identities of everyone who's listened to it.

Mining and transactions are the twin engines that power the Bitcoin network. They work in tandem to secure the network, process payments, and introduce new Bitcoins into the system, all without the oversight of a central authority. This decentralized approach is what makes Bitcoin revolutionary. It's a system built on trust, verification, and the collective effort of the community, much like a music scene where everyone plays a part in preserving and sharing the culture. So, whether you're mining for that next block or sending Bitcoins across the globe, you're contributing to a larger movement that's reshaping what money means in the digital age.

Venturing into the world of Bitcoin is akin to discovering a secret spot where you can enjoy your favorite pastimes with ease and freedom. It's about stepping away from the mainstream, finding a space that offers something more aligned with your values and lifestyle. Let's explore the advantages of Bitcoin, which make it not just a digital currency, but a revolution in how we think about and use money.

Lower Transaction Fees: Imagine planning a road trip to your favorite secluded spot. Traditionally, you'd expect tolls along the way, each taking a little from your travel fund. In the financial world, these are akin to the transaction fees charged by banks and online payment systems, which can add up, especially for international transfers. Bitcoin, in contrast, operates with significantly lower fees because it bypasses these traditional intermediaries. It's like finding a scenic, toll-free route to your destination, leaving more in your pocket for the things you love.

Anonymity and Privacy: In a world where every online move seems tracked and cataloged, Bitcoin offers a breath of fresh air. Transactions with Bitcoin provide a level of anonymity not available through other financial transactions. While it's not entirely anonymous (since transactions are recorded on the public blockchain), the parties involved are represented by addresses, not personal information. It's akin to enjoying your secret spot without leaving a sign-in log for everyone to see who was there and when — a layer of privacy in an increasingly transparent world.

Potential as an Investment: Investing in Bitcoin has been likened to investing in the internet in the early '90s — a new frontier with untold potential. Despite its volatility, Bitcoin has seen remarkable growth over the years, outperforming traditional investments like stocks and gold for certain periods. It's like discovering a rare vinyl record at a garage sale for pennies and finding out it's a collector's item worth thousands. The potential for significant returns is there, but it requires patience, research, and a willingness to ride the waves of the market.

Decentralization: One of Bitcoin's core advantages is its decentralized nature. There's no central authority, like a bank or government, controlling Bitcoin. This decentralization means users have full control over their transactions and funds. It's akin to creating a community garden where everyone has a say, and no single entity can decide what's grown or who gets to partake. This level of control and freedom is unprecedented in the traditional financial system.

Global Accessibility: Bitcoin is borderless. It enables transactions between individuals worldwide without the need for currency exchange or the involvement of banks. Imagine a world where you can send support to a friend halfway across the globe as easily as handing them cash in person, without worrying about exchange rates or bank fees. It's a global financial system that's as accessible as the internet itself.

Security: Thanks to the cryptographic underpinnings of the blockchain, Bitcoin offers a high level of security. Owning Bitcoin means holding a private key, a secure digital code known only to you and the blockchain. It's like having a digital safe where your digital gold is stored, protected from unauthorized access.

In embracing Bitcoin, you're not just choosing a new way to transact; you're participating in a movement towards a more accessible, private, and equitable financial system. It's about finding that hassle-free way to enjoy what matters most to you, without the traditional barriers and constraints. Bitcoin represents a path to financial freedom, a way to navigate the world on your terms, much like finding that perfect spot where you can relax and be yourself, undisturbed and free.

Embarking on a journey into the world of Bitcoin is much like setting out on a road trip to an uncharted destination. The excitement and promise of adventure are palpable, yet the path is not without its perils. As we cruise down the digital highway exploring the vast landscape of cryptocurrency, it's crucial to be aware of the bumps along the way. Understanding these risks and challenges is key to navigating the journey with confidence and arriving safely at your desired destination.

Volatility: If there's one word that captures the essence of Bitcoin's market, it's volatility. The price of Bitcoin can skyrocket to dizzying heights or plummet to sobering lows in the blink of an eye, much like the sudden twists and turns of a mountain road. This volatility stems from various factors, including market sentiment, news events, and shifts in regulatory landscapes. For the unprepared traveler, these fluctuations can be disorienting and even perilous. However, with the right mindset and strategies, volatility can also present opportunities for growth and learning. It requires a steady hand on the wheel and an eye on the horizon, ready to adapt to the changing conditions.

Security Concerns: As with any valuable asset, Bitcoin attracts its share of threats. Security concerns in the Bitcoin space range from hacking attempts on exchanges and wallets to the potential loss of private keys due to user error or technical mishaps. Think of these as the unpredictable weather conditions or roadblocks that can appear without warning on your journey. The decentralized nature of Bitcoin is both a blessing and a curse; while it provides freedom from centralized control, it also places the onus of security squarely on the shoulders of the individual. Safeguarding your digital assets requires diligence, akin to securing your belongings and vehicle against theft or damage. This includes using reputable wallets, enabling two-factor authentication, and practicing safe storage methods for private keys.

Regulatory Risks: Navigating the regulatory landscape of Bitcoin can be akin to traversing a road with constantly changing traffic laws. Governments and financial institutions around the world are still grappling with how to classify, regulate, and tax cryptocurrency. For travelers on the Bitcoin road, this can mean sudden detours or adjustments to their journey as new regulations come into effect. Staying informed and compliant with local laws is essential, requiring a level of alertness and flexibility to adapt to new rules.

Market Manipulation: The cryptocurrency market, with its relatively small size compared to traditional financial markets, is susceptible to manipulation by large players or coordinated groups. These manipulative practices can create artificial highs and lows, misleading the unwary traveler. Awareness and caution can help navigate these treacherous stretches, keeping an eye out for warning signs of manipulation and steering clear of too-good-to-be-true schemes.

Emotional Trading: Lastly, the journey through the Bitcoin landscape can be an emotional one. The thrill of a price surge or the panic of a drop can lead to rash decisions, driving travelers off their planned route. Emotional trading is a pitfall that can derail even the most seasoned adventurers. Cultivating a mindset of patience, discipline, and long-term planning is akin to preparing for all eventualities on a road trip, ensuring that emotions don't dictate the direction of travel.

Embarking on the Bitcoin journey, armed with knowledge of these risks and challenges, is like setting out on a road trip with a full tank, a reliable map, and a sense of adventure. It's about enjoying the journey, prepared for the bumps along the way, and ready to navigate the twists and turns of the road ahead. With preparation, caution, and a steady hand, the trip through the world of Bitcoin can be as rewarding as it is exhilarating.

In the genesis of the digital currency era, Bitcoin emerged not with a thunderous explosion but as a ripple in the vast ocean of the internet, barely noticed by the masses. Its early days were characterized by a blend of skepticism and intrigue, a novel concept too radical for many to grasp or take seriously. Imagine a seed planted in unfertile ground, its potential for growth underestimated by onlookers unfamiliar with the resilience of its roots. This was Bitcoin in its infancy, a revolutionary idea waiting to break through the surface.

The narrative of Bitcoin's early adoption is a tapestry woven with tales of visionaries and pioneers, individuals who saw beyond the skepticism to recognize the potential of a decentralized currency. Among these were tech enthusiasts, libertarians, and those disenchanted with the traditional banking system, all united by a belief in the power of blockchain technology to transform the financial landscape.

One of the most emblematic stories from these early days is the now-legendary pizza purchase. On May 22, 2010, a programmer named Laszlo Hanyecz made history by making the first real-world transaction using Bitcoin. He posted on a Bitcoin forum, offering 10,000 Bitcoins to anyone who could deliver two large pizzas to his house. A fellow forum user took up the offer, and the transaction was completed, valuing the two pizzas at what would be worth millions of dollars today. This event, now celebrated as Bitcoin Pizza Day, symbolized the first tangible proof of concept for Bitcoin's use as a currency and marked a pivotal moment in its journey from obscurity to mainstream awareness.

The early days also saw the creation of the first Bitcoin exchange, allowing people to trade Bitcoin and fiat currencies, laying the groundwork for the vibrant ecosystem that would follow. These platforms were rudimentary compared to today's sophisticated exchanges, but they provided an essential service, acting as bridges between the traditional financial system and this new digital frontier.

Skepticism persisted, however. Many dismissed Bitcoin as a fleeting trend, a geek's fantasy with no real-world application. Critics pointed to its volatility, its association with illicit online marketplaces, and the lack of regulatory oversight as insurmountable hurdles. Yet, with every challenge, the Bitcoin community grew stronger, its members united in their resolve to address these issues and to demonstrate the potential of decentralized finance.

Gradually, acceptance began to grow. Businesses started to see the value in a currency that offered low transaction fees, irreversible transactions, and anonymity. Tech-savvy consumers appreciated the control and security offered by a currency untethered to any nation-state or central bank. As more people began to use Bitcoin, its network effect grew, attracting even more users and further legitimizing its place in the digital economy.

The early days of Bitcoin were a time of experimentation, of trial and error, and of unwavering belief in the face of skepticism. Those early adopters and the notable transactions they undertook laid the foundation for the cryptocurrency revolution. Their stories are not just footnotes in the history of Bitcoin; they are testaments to the power of innovation, vision, and community in overcoming doubt and shaping the future of finance.

In the unfolding saga of Bitcoin, few chapters are as controversial yet undeniably pivotal as the rise of the Silk Road. Launched in February 2011, the Silk Road was an online marketplace, but not of the ordinary variety. Hidden in the dark web and accessible only through the Tor browser, which anonymizes web traffic, the Silk Road became the digital era's clandestine bazaar, a place where users could purchase anything from rare books to illicit substances, all in complete privacy.

The Silk Road didn't just push boundaries; it obliterated them, creating a space where the unregulated exchange of goods and services flourished. Its role in Bitcoin's history is monumental, serving as the first large-scale proof of concept for Bitcoin's use as a means of transaction. Here, Bitcoin found its first "killer app," a real-world application that demonstrated its utility beyond speculative investment or a topic of academic interest. The anonymity and security of Bitcoin transactions complemented the Silk Road's ethos of privacy and freedom, making Bitcoin the currency of choice for the marketplace's users.

The marketplace quickly gained notoriety, drawing the attention of not only those seeking its hidden offerings but also of policymakers and law enforcement agencies worldwide. To its proponents, the Silk Road was an embodiment of the libertarian ideals that underpinned Bitcoin's creation: a free market operating beyond government control, where individual autonomy and privacy were paramount. To its detractors, it was a nefarious underbelly of the internet, a place where illegal activities could thrive unchecked.

Despite the controversy, the Silk Road played an undeniable role in popularizing Bitcoin. It showcased the cryptocurrency's potential to facilitate transactions in a way that was previously not possible, highlighting Bitcoin's value proposition as a decentralized and anonymous currency. The marketplace brought Bitcoin into the spotlight, attracting a wave of new users and speculators and sparking a debate on the nature of money, privacy, and the role of state regulation in the digital age.

The eventual shutdown of the Silk Road by the FBI in October 2013 marked the end of an era but also the beginning of a new chapter for Bitcoin. While the marketplace's closure was a blow to those who saw it as a symbol of digital freedom, it also served to disentangle Bitcoin's image from illicit activities. In the aftermath, Bitcoin's resilience became apparent. Rather than collapsing, the ecosystem around it continued to grow, diversifying into legitimate businesses, exchanges, and applications that extended far beyond the Silk Road's shadow.

The legacy of the Silk Road in Bitcoin's history is complex. It stands as a testament to the disruptive power of technology to challenge existing norms and regulations. Just as underground movements have always pushed societal boundaries, challenging us to rethink our values and laws, the Silk Road challenged the world to reconsider the essence of commerce, privacy, and regulation in an increasingly digital world. It underscored Bitcoin's role not just as a currency but as a catalyst for debate and change, setting the stage for the next evolution of the internet's financial infrastructure.

Navigating through the annals of Bitcoin's history, one can draw parallels to the evolution of a groundbreaking musical genre, marked by pivotal albums and transformative events that not only define its trajectory but also its influence on the broader cultural landscape. Bitcoin, since its inception, has charted a course through uncharted territories, experiencing both meteoric rises and steep declines, facing regulatory scrutiny, and witnessing the birth of a whole new ecosystem of digital currencies. These milestones, much like landmark albums, have punctuated Bitcoin's journey, each contributing to the narrative of this digital revolution.

The First Price Surge: The early days of Bitcoin saw its value as more of a curiosity than a legitimate financial asset. However, in April 2013, Bitcoin's price surged to over $250, marking its arrival on the global stage as something more than an internet oddity. This moment was akin to a debut album that breaks through to mainstream recognition, challenging perceptions and setting the stage for future success.

The Mt. Gox Saga: Once the world's largest Bitcoin exchange, Mt. Gox's collapse in 2014 due to a massive hack was a moment of reckoning. It was Bitcoin's equivalent of a controversial band breakup, a pivotal event that tested the resilience of the community and the integrity of the ecosystem. Despite the setback, the aftermath led to increased calls for regulation and the implementation of stronger security measures across exchanges.

Regulatory Battles and Recognition: Bitcoin's journey has been marked by its encounters with regulatory bodies worldwide. In some cases, it faced outright bans, while in others, it received cautious acceptance. The most significant acknowledgment came in 2017 when Japan recognized Bitcoin as a legal payment method. These regulatory milestones shaped the environment within which Bitcoin operates, much like landmark legislation or court rulings that have defined the boundaries of artistic expression and intellectual property in music.

The 2017 Bull Run: The year 2017 stands out in Bitcoin's history as the year of its most dramatic bull run, with its price soaring to nearly $20,000 by December. This unprecedented surge was Bitcoin's blockbuster hit, its "Thriller" or "Dark Side of the Moon," capturing the world's attention and forever altering the landscape of cryptocurrency investment.

The Emergence of Competitors: Just as successful genres give rise to subgenres and inspired contemporaries, Bitcoin's success paved the way for a plethora of other cryptocurrencies, each with its unique features and value propositions. Ethereum, Ripple, Litecoin, and others entered the scene, creating a diverse ecosystem that expanded the possibilities of blockchain technology beyond simple currency transactions.

Institutional Adoption and the Mainstreaming of Bitcoin: Recent years have seen Bitcoin embraced by traditional financial institutions, with futures trading, ETF proposals, and major corporations adding Bitcoin to their balance sheets. This phase of Bitcoin's journey mirrors the moment when a niche genre gains mainstream acceptance, influencing everything from fashion to film, and cementing its place in cultural history.

Through these milestones, Bitcoin has undergone a transformation from an obscure digital experiment to a major financial asset, influencing not just the world of finance but also societal notions of value, privacy, and autonomy. Each milestone, with its challenges and triumphs, has been a note in the symphony of Bitcoin's history, contributing to its enduring legacy and its place in the digital age's cultural zeitgeist.

In the vibrant history of Bitcoin, a series of visionaries, innovators, and rebels have emerged, each playing a pivotal role in shaping its journey. Like the rock stars and icons of music who leave an indelible mark on their genres, these individuals have contributed their unique genius to the Bitcoin saga, pushing boundaries and challenging the status quo. Their stories add depth and color to the narrative of Bitcoin, embodying the spirit of innovation and resistance that defines the cryptocurrency movement.

Satoshi Nakamoto: The enigmatic founder of Bitcoin, Satoshi Nakamoto, is the mythical figurehead of the cryptocurrency world, akin to a legendary artist whose early work inspires a whole new genre of music. Much like Bob Dylan catalyzed the folk-rock movement, Satoshi's creation of Bitcoin and the blockchain technology underpinning it has ignited a financial revolution. Despite their anonymity and eventual withdrawal from the project, Satoshi's initial writings and the Bitcoin software they released to the world laid the groundwork for a decentralized future, making them a figure of endless fascination and respect within the community.

Hal Finney: Among the first to respond to Satoshi's call to action, Hal Finney is a revered pioneer in the Bitcoin community. A renowned cryptographer and one of the first people to conduct a Bitcoin transaction (with Satoshi themselves), Finney's contributions to Bitcoin's early development are monumental. His enthusiasm and technical expertise helped to steer Bitcoin through its infancy, much like a seasoned producer guiding a young band through their first recording session. Despite battling illness, Finney remained a passionate advocate for Bitcoin until his passing, leaving behind a legacy of innovation and dedication.

Nick Szabo: Often speculated to be one of the individuals behind the pseudonym Satoshi Nakamoto (though he has denied it), Nick Szabo is a polymath whose work on digital contracts and currencies laid the intellectual groundwork for Bitcoin. His concept of "bit gold" in the late 1990s and early 2000s is considered a precursor to Bitcoin. Szabo's contributions to the field of cryptography and digital currency are akin to a pioneering artist who blends genres, pushing music into uncharted territories.

Vitalik Buterin: While not a founder of Bitcoin, Vitalik Buterin has played a crucial role in the broader cryptocurrency narrative through the creation of Ethereum, a blockchain platform that extended the possibilities of Satoshi's original vision. Buterin's work introduced the concept of smart contracts, opening up new avenues for decentralized applications (dApps). His vision for Ethereum has made it the second most valuable cryptocurrency platform after Bitcoin, much like a breakthrough second album that confirms the staying power of a new musical act.

Charlie Shrem: A Bitcoin entrepreneur and advocate, Charlie Shrem founded one of the first Bitcoin exchanges, BitInstant, in 2011. His early efforts to bring Bitcoin into the mainstream and his subsequent legal troubles mirror the classic tale of a rock star's meteoric rise and fall. Despite facing adversity, Shrem remains a vocal proponent of Bitcoin and cryptocurrencies, embodying the resilience and rebellious spirit that characterizes much of the Bitcoin community.

Andreas Antonopoulos: An articulate and passionate advocate for Bitcoin, Andreas Antonopoulos has played a vital role in educating people about Bitcoin and blockchain technology. Through his books, speeches, and podcasts, Antonopoulos has demystified complex concepts and inspired countless individuals to explore and adopt Bitcoin. His contributions are reminiscent of an influential critic or journalist in the music world, whose insights and advocacy bring attention to emerging genres and artists.

Each of these figures, with their unique contributions and journeys, has helped to shape the world of Bitcoin and cryptocurrencies. Like the rock stars and rebels of the financial world, they have challenged conventional norms, explored new frontiers, and in doing so, have played integral roles in the ongoing saga of Bitcoin.

Market volatility, in its essence, is the financial world's version of weather patterns in the realm of agriculture. Just as a seasoned farmer understands that growing seasons come with their inherent unpredictability—droughts, storms, and unseasonably warm or cool temperatures—traders and investors in the Bitcoin market navigate a landscape marked by rapid price changes and unpredictable market movements. This volatility can be as exhilarating as the first warm day of spring, inviting new growth and opportunities, or as daunting as an unexpected frost, challenging even the most seasoned participants to adapt quickly.

In the Bitcoin market, this volatility is particularly pronounced, much like the microclimate of a delicate vineyard where the finest grapes are grown. Several factors contribute to these conditions, creating an environment ripe for both opportunity and caution. For one, Bitcoin's relatively small market size, compared to traditional financial markets, means that trades of significant volume can cause substantial price movements, akin to a heavy rainstorm flooding a parched field.

Moreover, the Bitcoin market operates 24/7, without the traditional opening and closing bells of stock exchanges. This continuous trading cycle is like a farm that never sleeps, where conditions can change dramatically overnight, requiring constant vigilance and readiness to act.

The novelty of Bitcoin and the evolving regulatory landscape also add layers of uncertainty, reminiscent of the introduction of a new crop to a region. Just as farmers must learn to adapt to the needs of a new plant, navigating unforeseen challenges and learning from each season, Bitcoin traders and investors must stay informed and adaptable, ready to respond to regulatory changes, technological advancements, and shifts in investor sentiment.

Additionally, the sentiment-driven nature of the Bitcoin market amplifies its volatility. Just as a sudden heatwave can send farmers scrambling to protect their crops, news events, social media buzz, and market trends can send Bitcoin prices soaring or plummeting in a matter of hours. This high sensitivity to sentiment highlights the emotional and psychological aspects of trading, underscoring the need for patience, discipline, and a well-considered strategy.

Understanding the nature of Bitcoin's volatility is akin to respecting the unpredictability of the seasons. It requires an appreciation of the underlying factors that contribute to market movements, a recognition of the risks involved, and an acknowledgment of the need for patience and adaptability. Just as farmers look to the sky and adjust their strategies accordingly, so too must Bitcoin traders and investors remain vigilant, ready to adapt their approaches in response to the market's ever-changing landscape.

Navigating the Bitcoin market's volatility is akin to preparing for a season's harvest, where a myriad of factors, like unpredictable weather patterns, can significantly impact the outcome. In the realm of Bitcoin, these elements include regulatory news, technological developments, and market sentiment, each playing a critical role in shaping the market's ebbs and flows. Understanding these factors is like reading the signs of impending weather changes, allowing those involved to brace for impact or capitalize on favorable conditions.

Regulatory News: Just as a sudden storm can flood fields or a drought can parch the earth, regulatory announcements can send shockwaves through the Bitcoin market. Changes in legislation, policy statements from financial authorities, or government actions against digital currencies in various countries are akin to unpredictable weather patterns that can either nourish the market or stunt its growth. For instance, when a major economy announces a crackdown on cryptocurrency, it's like an unexpected frost, chilling the market. Conversely, regulatory clarity or support can function as a much-needed rain shower, revitalizing the market and encouraging growth.

Technological Developments: The Bitcoin ecosystem is continually evolving, with technological advancements playing a pivotal role in its growth and stability. The introduction of new features, security enhancements, and scalability solutions is comparable to the development of more resilient crop varieties or innovative farming techniques. These improvements can lead to increased adoption and stability, much like a bountiful harvest after implementing better farming practices. However, technological setbacks or the emergence of competing cryptocurrencies can disrupt the market, similar to a pest infestation that threatens crops, requiring quick adaptation and problem-solving.

Market Sentiment: Perhaps the most capricious of all factors, market sentiment can shift with the wind, driven by news, rumors, and investor behavior. This sentiment, whether bullish or bearish, acts like the daily weather, influencing trading behavior on a day-to-day basis. Positive news or hype can create a sunny climate for Bitcoin, driving prices up as enthusiasm grows. Conversely, negative news or fear can cast clouds over the market, leading to price drops as investors seek shelter. The emotional and psychological aspects of trading, fueled by media reports and social media, contribute to rapid changes in sentiment, making the market's mood as variable as a summer day's weather.

Understanding these influencing factors requires not just a keen eye on the market but also an awareness of the broader world, much like a farmer must pay attention to both the condition of their fields and the changing seasons. Regulatory shifts, technological progress, and shifts in sentiment are interwoven, affecting each other and the market in complex ways. For those navigating the Bitcoin market, staying informed and adaptable, ready to respond to these changes, is crucial. It's about reading the signs, preparing for the unexpected, and seizing opportunities when conditions align, much like the eternal dance of the farmer with the whims of nature, always striving for a fruitful harvest amidst the uncertainty of the changing seasons.

Coping with the volatility of the Bitcoin market is akin to navigating the highs and lows of a psychedelic journey. It requires a balanced mindset, a supportive community, and strategies that anchor you to your long-term vision, helping you ride out the waves without succumbing to panic. Here are some strategies to weather the storm, drawing parallels to maintaining composure and clarity during a challenging experience.

Maintain a Long-term Perspective: Just as a seasoned psychonaut understands that each phase of a trip is temporary and contributes to a larger journey, Bitcoin investors should keep their eyes on the horizon. The market's volatility is less daunting when viewed as part of Bitcoin's broader evolution. By focusing on long-term goals and the fundamental reasons for investing in Bitcoin, you can avoid being swayed by short-term fluctuations. This approach is like focusing on the growth and insights gained from a challenging experience, rather than getting caught up in momentary discomfort.

Diversification: In the same way that a varied playlist can guide you through different moods and settings during a trip, diversifying your investment portfolio can help smooth out the volatility of the market. By spreading investments across different asset classes (not just within the crypto space but also in traditional markets), you can mitigate the impact of a downturn in any single investment. Diversification doesn't eliminate risk, but it's like having different perspectives and tools at your disposal, each contributing to a more balanced and resilient overall experience.

Avoid Panic Selling: Panic selling during a market downturn is akin to trying to escape a bad trip by fighting against it, which often only intensifies the discomfort. Instead, just as you would ground yourself and breathe through a challenging moment, take a step back during market dips. Assess whether anything has fundamentally changed with your investment thesis. Often, the best course of action is to hold steady, recalling that markets move in cycles, and what goes down often comes back up. Support from investment communities or financial advisors during these times can serve as a calming influence, much like the reassuring presence of friends during a tough trip.

Regular Review and Adjustment: Staying informed and being willing to adjust your strategy is crucial. This doesn't mean reacting to every market movement, but rather periodically reviewing your portfolio to ensure it still aligns with your goals and risk tolerance. Think of it as checking your bearings during a journey, making sure you're still on the path you want to be on. Just as you might change your environment or music to shift the direction of a trip, adjusting your investments in response to significant changes in the market or your life can help keep you on track.

Education and Mindfulness: Finally, educating yourself about the Bitcoin market and the factors that influence its movements can provide a sense of control and preparedness. Knowledge is power, and understanding the historical trends of market cycles can demystify volatility, making it less intimidating. This is similar to the way learning about the effects of psychedelics can prepare you for the experience, reducing anxiety and fear. Mindfulness and stress-reduction techniques can also be beneficial, helping you maintain a calm and centered mindset, regardless of market conditions.

Coping with Bitcoin's volatility is not about avoiding the waves but learning to surf them. By adopting a long-term perspective, diversifying your investments, resisting the urge to panic sell, staying informed, and making mindful adjustments, you can navigate the market's ups and downs with confidence. Just as a challenging trip can lead to personal growth and insight with the right mindset and support, so too can the volatile journey of Bitcoin investing yield positive outcomes for those who approach it with patience, wisdom, and resilience.

The swirling mists of volatility in the Bitcoin market, often viewed with trepidation, can also be a fertile ground for opportunities for those who are prepared. Like a seasoned forager who knows that the most tumultuous climates can yield the rarest seeds, savvy investors can navigate the market's unpredictability to their advantage. Understanding that volatility isn't just a challenge but also a potential boon requires a shift in perspective and strategy, akin to recognizing the value in what others might overlook.

Buying the Dip: One of the most straightforward strategies in a volatile market is to "buy the dip." When prices plummet, it can be an opportune moment to acquire assets at a lower price, before a potential rebound. This approach is like finding a rare seedling or bulb at the end of the season; it may seem inconsequential at the moment, but with care and patience, it can grow into something extraordinary. The key is to have a solid understanding of the market and the assets in question, ensuring that the decision to buy is based on more than just the thrill of the hunt.

D   ollar-Cost Averaging: Volatility can make timing the market an incredibly challenging task. Dollar-cost averaging (DCA) is a strategy that mitigates this issue by spreading out investments over time, purchasing a fixed dollar amount of a particular asset on a regular schedule, regardless of its price. This method can be likened to planting a variety of seeds throughout different seasons, knowing that while some may not thrive, the overall diversity and timing can lead to a bountiful harvest over time.

Strategic Selling: Just as important as knowing when to acquire assets is understanding when to let them go. Volatility can create rapid price increases, presenting opportunities to sell for those who are ready. This doesn't necessarily mean exiting a position entirely but perhaps pruning a portfolio to realize profits or rebalance assets. Like a gardener who selectively harvests crops at just the right time, knowing when to sell requires an intimate understanding of the market's seasons and cycles.

Hedging: In the realm of investment, hedging involves taking an opposing position in a related asset to offset potential losses. This can be particularly useful in volatile markets, acting as a form of insurance against sudden downturns. For the agricultural enthusiast, this is akin to planting a crop known to be resilient to certain adverse conditions alongside more sensitive varieties, ensuring that no matter what the season brings, there is something to harvest.

Leveraging Technology: Finally, the use of technology can empower investors to seize opportunities in a volatile market. Automated trading algorithms, for instance, can execute trades based on predefined criteria, capitalizing on fluctuations that occur faster than a human can react. This approach is like employing a sophisticated irrigation system that responds dynamically to changes in weather, ensuring that crops receive exactly what they need, exactly when they need it.

Embracing volatility as an opportunity requires preparation, a keen eye for patterns, and a willingness to act decisively yet thoughtfully. It's about cultivating a garden in an unpredictable climate, armed with the knowledge and tools to take advantage of every rain shower and sunny day. For those who navigate these waters with skill and foresight, the volatile world of Bitcoin offers not just challenges, but a landscape rich with potential for growth and reward.

Chapter 2

Rolling into Crypto

Setting Up Your Digital Wallet

Venturing into the world of cryptocurrency, one of the first steps on your journey is securing a reliable and suitable digital wallet. Imagine embarking on a grand adventure or a prolonged trek into nature. Just as you'd need the right kind of bag to carry your essentials, tailored to the nature of your journey—be it a rugged backpack for mountainous treks or a sleek suitcase for city travel—a digital wallet serves as your essential gear in the vast and varied terrain of the crypto world.

What Are Digital Wallets?

Digital wallets are not so different from your physical wallet, where you stash your cash and cards. However, instead of holding physical currency, they store cryptographic information—private keys and public addresses—that allows you to access, send, and receive cryptocurrency. They act as a bridge to the blockchain, enabling you to interact with your digital assets. Each wallet type offers different features, levels of security, and convenience, catering to various needs and preferences in the cryptocurrency ecosystem.

Types of Digital Wallets

Hardware Wallets: Like a secure, portable safe, hardware wallets are physical devices that store your private keys offline. They are immune to online hacking attempts, making them one of the safest options. Hardware wallets are ideal for those holding significant amounts of cryptocurrency and who prioritize security above all. Think of it as the heavy-duty, lockable trunk for your most valuable treasures.

Software Wallets: These wallets run on your computer or another device, storing your private keys digitally. They can be further divided into:

Desktop Wallets: Installed on a personal computer, offering a balance of convenience and security. It's akin to a trusty backpack that keeps your items reasonably safe, provided you don't leave it unattended in public spaces.

Mobile Wallets: Run on smartphones, making your crypto easily accessible and allowing you to transact on the go. Imagine a versatile crossbody bag, perfect for quick access and day trips but not ideal for storing all your valuables.

Web Wallets: Operated through a browser interface, they can be accessed from any device. While extremely convenient, they often store your private keys online, which can pose a risk. This is like a lightweight tote bag; it's perfect for everyday essentials but not the best choice for valuable or sensitive items.

Paper Wallets: Essentially a physical document that contains your public address and private key, often in the form of QR codes. While paper wallets are immune to digital hacking, they are susceptible to physical damage and loss. Consider this the envelope system of cryptocurrency—simple and surprisingly effective for storage but requires careful handling and isn't practical for frequent transactions.

Function and Importance

Digital wallets are more than just storage; they are your personal interface with the cryptocurrency network, enabling you to manage your investments, make transactions, and interact with decentralized applications. Choosing the right wallet is akin to selecting the perfect bag for your adventure; it needs to match your activity level, provide adequate protection for your items, and suit your style of travel.

As you prepare to dive into the digital currency space, understanding the nuances of each wallet type will empower you to make informed decisions, ensuring that your crypto journey is both exhilarating and secure. Just as the right bag can enhance your travel experience, the right digital wallet can significantly influence your journey through the crypto landscape, making it smoother, safer, and more enjoyable.

As you delve into the world of cryptocurrencies, selecting the right digital wallet is akin to choosing the best method to store and enjoy your favorite strains or records. Each type of wallet comes with its unique set of features, advantages, and drawbacks, much like how vinyl enthusiasts decide between shelves, cases, or digital archives for their music collections. Let's explore the diverse landscape of digital wallets, understanding their nuances to help you make an informed choice that resonates with your lifestyle and investment strategy.

Hardware Wallets: The Safety Deposit Box

Pros: Hardware wallets are like the safety deposit boxes for your digital currency. They store your private keys offline on a physical device, making them virtually impervious to online hacking attempts. Ideal for substantial investments, they offer peace of mind, much like securely storing a rare, vintage record in a climate-controlled environment to preserve its value and integrity.

Cons: The primary drawback is their cost, as they represent an upfront investment. Additionally, their physical nature means they can be lost or damaged, and retrieving assets from a damaged or lost hardware wallet can be challenging. They're not as convenient for quick, daily transactions, akin to needing to visit the bank vault every time you want to listen to a particular record.

Desktop Wallets: The Home Library

Pros: Desktop wallets offer a balance between security and accessibility, running on your personal computer and storing your keys offline when not in use. They're like having a personal library of records at home—safe, as long as your home is secure, and readily accessible whenever you wish.

Cons: Their security is contingent on the security of your computer. If your computer gets hacked, infected with malware, or suffers a hardware failure, your assets are at risk. It's similar to the risk of your records getting damaged or stolen if your home security is compromised.

Mobile Wallets: The Daily Carry

Pros: Mobile wallets bring convenience to the forefront, allowing you to carry your crypto in your pocket for everyday use. It's like having a digital music player or a portable case for a few favorite records, ready to share or enjoy at any moment.

Cons: This convenience comes with increased risk. Mobile devices are more likely to be lost, stolen, or accessed via unsecured internet connections. The security of your assets in a mobile wallet is as variable as the places you bring your phone.

Web Wallets: The Streaming Service

Pros: Web wallets offer unparalleled convenience, accessible from any internet-connected device. They're the streaming service of digital wallets, allowing you to access your crypto anywhere, anytime, without needing to carry a physical device or download software.

Cons: This convenience comes at the expense of security. Since your keys are stored online, they're vulnerable to hacking. Using a web wallet is akin to streaming music—you get easy access but at the risk of lower quality (security) and the potential for service interruptions (hacks).

Paper Wallets: The Vinyl Record

Pros: Paper wallets are a form of cold storage, providing an offline method to store your crypto keys on a physical document. They're like vinyl records—tangible, offline, and carry a certain nostalgia. They're immune to digital attacks and represent a piece of the blockchain that you can hold in your hands.

Cons: However, like a vinyl record, they're susceptible to physical wear and tear, loss, and damage. Moreover, using a paper wallet requires a higher level of knowledge to ensure secure transactions, akin to the care needed to maintain and play vinyl records without damaging them.

Each wallet type serves a different need, mirroring the variety of ways one might choose to store and enjoy music or any collectible. Your choice depends on the balance you wish to strike between security and convenience, the volume of your transactions, and your lifestyle. Whether you prefer the security of a hardware wallet, the convenience of a web wallet, or the tangibility of a paper wallet, understanding these options allows you to navigate the crypto space with confidence, much like a connoisseur selects the perfect storage method for their prized possessions.

Choosing the right digital wallet is akin to selecting the perfect vehicle for a road trip. Just as you'd weigh various factors like fuel efficiency, comfort, terrain capability, and storage space depending on your destination and travel style, selecting a digital wallet requires a thoughtful consideration of security, convenience, accessibility, and the types of cryptocurrencies it supports. Each of these factors plays a crucial role in ensuring that your journey into the crypto world is as smooth and enjoyable as your adventures on the open road.

Security: The cornerstone of any good wallet, security is like the safety features of a vehicle. Just as you'd look for airbags, anti-lock brakes, and a sturdy frame to protect you on your journey, a wallet's security measures protect your digital assets from theft and unauthorized access. Consider what security features are offered, such as two-factor authentication, multi-signature support, and backup and recovery options. It's about finding the right balance between Fort Knox-level security and practical usability, much like choosing a vehicle with the best safety ratings without it being a tank.

Convenience: Convenience in a digital wallet is like the usability of a car's interior features. It should be user-friendly, allowing you easy access to your funds when you need them, just as a car's navigation system, cup holders, and comfortable seating make a long drive more enjoyable. For daily transactions, a mobile or web wallet might be your go-to, offering the ease of access akin to a reliable sedan with all the tech comforts. For long-term storage, however, a hardware wallet, though less convenient for frequent access, might be the equivalent of an off-road vehicle equipped for rugged terrain, offering peace of mind over smooth daily operation.

Accessibility: This refers to how easily you can access your wallet from different devices or locations. Like a vehicle's fuel efficiency that determines how far and often you can travel without a refill, a wallet's accessibility affects how easily you can manage your crypto assets on the go. A web or mobile wallet scores high on accessibility, similar to an electric car with fast charging capability, allowing you quick and easy access. However, remember that increased accessibility can sometimes compromise security, much like how faster cars might offer less protection in a crash.

Support for Different Cryptocurrencies: Just as a versatile SUV can navigate city streets, mountain roads, and desert paths, a wallet that supports a wide range of cryptocurrencies offers you the flexibility to diversify your portfolio without needing multiple wallets. Consider your investment strategy and whether you plan to stick with Bitcoin or explore other altcoins. A multi-currency wallet is like having an all-terrain vehicle, ready for any adventure, whereas a Bitcoin-only wallet might be akin to a specialized sports car, perfect for its specific purpose but limited in versatility.

In your quest for the perfect digital wallet, consider these factors carefully, weighing each against your personal needs and goals in the crypto space. Just as selecting the right vehicle can make or break a road trip, choosing the right wallet can greatly influence your experience in the world of cryptocurrency. Whether you prioritize the rugged security of a hardware wallet, the sleek convenience of a mobile wallet, or the all-terrain capability of a multi-currency wallet, ensure your choice aligns with your journey ahead, fueling your crypto adventures with confidence and ease.

Venturing into the realm of cryptocurrency necessitates a foundational understanding of the security principles that keep your digital assets safe. At the heart of crypto security are concepts akin to everyday safety measures you already practice, such as locking your doors or keeping your personal identification secure. Let's demystify cryptographic security, private keys, and public addresses by drawing parallels to these familiar routines.

Cryptographic Security: Think of cryptographic security as the sophisticated lock on your front door, but instead of a metal key, it uses complex mathematical algorithms to lock and unlock information. Just as a high-quality lock prevents unauthorized access to your home, cryptographic techniques protect your digital assets by ensuring that transactions are secure and authenticated. It's like having a lock that can only be opened with a secret mathematical formula instead of a physical key, making it nearly impossible for intruders to break in.

Private Keys: Your private key in the world of cryptocurrency is akin to the house key you carry on your keychain. It's a unique, secret sequence of numbers and letters that you use to access and manage your cryptocurrency holdings. Just as you wouldn't share your house key with strangers or leave it lying around where someone could find it, your private key must be kept secure and confidential at all times. Losing your private key or letting it fall into the wrong hands is like giving someone free access to everything you hold dear inside your home.

Public Addresses: On the flip side, your public address is like your home's mailing address. It's the information you can share with others so they can send you cryptocurrency, much like how someone can send you a letter or parcel to your home address. Your public address lets you receive transactions without exposing your private key, just as your home address allows you to receive mail without giving everyone a key to your door. It's a way to interact with the world securely, ensuring that you can receive what's yours without compromising your safety.

Understanding these concepts is crucial as you navigate the crypto space. Just as you instinctively protect your physical keys and personal information in your everyday life, so too must you guard your private keys and understand the function of your public address in the digital realm. By applying the principles of personal safety to your digital assets, you can secure your cryptocurrency effectively, ensuring that your venture into this innovative landscape is both rewarding and safe.

Just as maintaining a healthy lifestyle involves regular habits and practices to keep your body and mind in top shape, securing your cryptocurrency requires a set of routine practices to safeguard your digital assets. Here's a guide to some of the best security practices, paralleled with the essential elements of a healthy lifestyle, ensuring that your venture into cryptocurrency is secure and prosperous.

Creating Strong Passwords: Think of creating a strong password like choosing a balanced diet. Just as a varied diet provides the nutrients your body needs, a complex password combines letters, numbers, and symbols to create a robust barrier against unauthorized access. Avoid common words or easy-to-guess combinations, much like steering clear of processed foods that offer little nutritional value. For the best security, use a unique password for each account, similar to how a well-rounded diet diversifies its sources of vitamins and minerals.

Securing Private Keys: Your private key is akin to the core of your physical health. Just as you might keep a health journal or a list of medications confidential and safe, your private key should be kept in a secure location—whether that's a hardware wallet, a securely encrypted digital file, or a safety deposit box. Consider making backups of your private key, similar to how you might have emergency contacts in case of a health issue. These backups should be kept in separate, equally secure locations to ensure you can always access your assets if one copy is lost or damaged.

Using Two-Factor Authentication (2FA): Enabling 2FA on your accounts is like adding a routine workout to your daily schedule. It provides an additional layer of security, much like how regular exercise strengthens your body against illnesses. With 2FA, accessing your account requires something you know (your password) and something you have (a code generated by your phone or a hardware token), significantly reducing the risk of unauthorized access. Just as a consistent exercise regimen builds resilience, using 2FA consistently fortifies your digital security posture.

Regularly Updating Software: Keeping your software up to date is similar to regular health check-ups. Just as you visit the doctor to catch any potential issues early, updating your wallet software, computer operating system, and security software ensures that you are protected against known vulnerabilities and threats. Developers continuously work to improve security features and fix bugs, so regular updates are critical to maintaining a secure environment for your digital assets.

Adopting these security practices is crucial for anyone venturing into the cryptocurrency space. Just as a healthy lifestyle requires attention to diet, exercise, and preventive care, securing your cryptocurrency involves diligence, caution, and a proactive approach to digital hygiene. By incorporating these habits into your routine, you can protect your digital wealth as effectively as you safeguard your physical and mental well-being.

Navigating the digital world of cryptocurrency, much like moving through various social situations in everyday life, requires an awareness of potential threats and the knowledge of how to avoid them. Just as you might encounter individuals or situations that could lead to undesirable outcomes, in the realm of cryptocurrency, threats like phishing scams, malware, and social engineering attacks are the digital equivalents, aiming to deceive or manipulate you for unauthorized access to your assets. Understanding these threats and how to safeguard against them is akin to learning how to navigate complex social environments safely.

Phishing Scams: Phishing scams are deceptive attempts to steal sensitive information through emails, websites, or messages that appear to be from legitimate sources. Imagine being at a party and someone convincingly pretending to be a friend of a friend, asking for the keys to your car or house. Just as you'd be cautious about verifying their identity and intentions, you should scrutinize emails and messages for signs of phishing. Look for unusual sender addresses, misspellings, or requests for sensitive information. Always verify the authenticity of a request by contacting the company directly through official channels, rather than clicking on links provided in suspicious messages.

Malware: Malware, or malicious software, can infect your device to steal information or damage your system. It's akin to accepting a seemingly harmless gift at a social gathering that turns out to be a trojan horse, hiding something harmful. Protect yourself by not downloading attachments or clicking on links from unknown sources, much like you'd exercise caution with anything handed to you by strangers. Regularly update your antivirus software and enable firewalls to detect and block threats, just as you'd stay informed about social cues and boundaries to avoid unwanted situations.

Social Engineering Attacks: These attacks exploit human psychology to trick individuals into breaking security protocols. Comparable to someone using peer pressure or manipulation to convince you to divulge personal information or make a risky decision at a social event, social engineering in the digital world can be equally persuasive. Attackers might impersonate authority figures or create scenarios that urge immediate action. Safeguard against these by verifying requests through independent means and taking a moment to assess the situation critically, much like taking a step back to evaluate the consequences in a high-pressure social setting.

Preventive Measures: Just as awareness and precaution can prevent awkward or harmful situations in social contexts, adopting a mindset of caution and skepticism online can protect you against digital threats. Educate yourself about the latest scams, use secure and unique passwords, and enable two-factor authentication on your accounts. Share knowledge with friends and family, as spreading awareness can create a community that's collectively more secure.

Understanding these threats and implementing strategies to avoid them does not mean living in fear but rather navigating the crypto space with informed confidence. Just as you'd learn to handle social interactions with grace and awareness, dealing with the potential pitfalls of the cryptocurrency world becomes manageable and routine, allowing you to focus on the opportunities and interactions that enrich your digital and physical life.

Understanding the fundamentals of crypto transactions is crucial for anyone entering the digital currency space, akin to mastering the art of sending a valuable package through the mail. Just as you'd take care to correctly address, securely package, and choose the right tracking options for a parcel, managing crypto transactions involves attention to wallet addresses, transaction fees, and the verification process to ensure your digital assets safely reach their intended destination.

Wallet Addresses: In the world of cryptocurrency, wallet addresses play a role similar to postal addresses in the mailing system. A wallet address is a unique string of letters and numbers that indicates the destination (or origin) for a crypto transaction. Just as you'd double-check the mailing address on a package to ensure it reaches the right person, verifying the accuracy of a wallet address is crucial for the successful transfer of digital currencies. Sending crypto to the wrong address can be like mailing a package to the wrong house—once it's gone, it's nearly impossible to retrieve.

Transaction Fees: When you send crypto, you'll often encounter transaction fees, which are akin to postage costs. These fees compensate the network participants (miners or validators) for processing and verifying transactions on the blockchain. Just as the cost of mailing a package can vary based on its size, weight, and how quickly you want it to arrive, transaction fees can fluctuate based on the blockchain network's congestion and the urgency of your transaction. Opting to pay a higher fee can be like choosing express delivery, ensuring your transaction is processed more quickly in times of high demand.

The Verification Process: After a transaction is initiated, it must be verified by the network—a process that ensures its validity and records it on the blockchain, similar to how a package is scanned and tracked at various points until delivery. This verification is performed by network nodes through a consensus mechanism, such as proof of work or proof of stake. It's as if each checkpoint your package passes through not only confirms its route but also secures its journey against tampering or loss, ensuring it arrives as intended.

Just as sending a valuable package requires trust in the postal service to deliver it based on the systems and safeguards in place, executing a crypto transaction relies on the underlying blockchain technology to securely and accurately process the transfer of digital assets. By understanding these basics—wallet addresses, transaction fees, and the verification process—you can navigate the crypto space with greater confidence, ensuring your digital assets are managed and transferred with the same care and precision as the most precious of parcels.

Transferring cryptocurrency can be likened to hosting a successful gathering; both require meticulous attention to detail, careful preparation, and a step-by-step approach to ensure everything goes smoothly. Here's a practical guide, akin to a recipe, for sending and receiving crypto that ensures a seamless transaction, much like ensuring a memorable and enjoyable time for your guests.

Ingredients (What You'll Need):

A secure digital wallet with cryptocurrency.

The recipient's wallet address.

Internet connection.

Instructions:

Step 1: Preparation

For Sending: Ensure your wallet is funded with enough cryptocurrency for the transfer, including transaction fees. It's like making sure you have enough ingredients before you start cooking.

For Receiving: Provide the sender with your wallet address. It's akin to giving clear directions to your home so guests can find it easily.

Step 2: Double-Check the Wallet Address

Just as you would carefully review your guest list to avoid leaving anyone out, meticulously verify the recipient's wallet address. A single mistake could send your crypto into the void, unrecoverable. If possible, use a secure method like an encrypted message or a phone call to confirm the address.

Step 3: Enter Details

In your wallet app, select the option to send crypto, and enter the recipient's address. Decide on the amount you wish to send. This step is like setting your table; everything must be placed just right for the event to proceed smoothly.

Step 4: Adjust Transaction Fees

Most wallets will suggest a fee, but this often can be adjusted. Higher fees can speed up the transaction, similar to choosing a premium delivery service for quicker shipping. Consider the network activity and urgency of your transaction, much like planning for potential traffic when deciding when to leave for an event.

Step 5: Review and Confirm

Carefully review all details, much like giving your home one last check before guests arrive. Ensure the address, amount, and fees are correct. Confirm the transaction once you're satisfied everything is in order.

Step 6: Transaction in Progress

Once confirmed, your transaction will be broadcast to the network, awaiting verification. This period of waiting is akin to the anticipation felt after guests are invited but before they arrive.

Step 7: Confirmation

After the network verifies the transaction, it will be finalized and recorded on the blockchain. You and the recipient will typically receive a confirmation. This is the moment your guests have arrived, and the gathering can truly begin.

Step 8: Celebrate and Follow-up

With the transaction complete, you've successfully sent or received cryptocurrency. Just as you'd follow up with guests after a party to thank them for coming and share memories, consider keeping a record of your transaction details for future reference.

Additional Tips:

Security: Just as you'd lock your home during a party, ensure your device and internet connection are secure when transacting.

Privacy: Be mindful of sharing your wallet address publicly, akin to not posting your home address openly on social media.

Patience: Sometimes, the network can be congested, and transactions may take longer, much like guests delayed in traffic. Keep an eye on the transaction status, but give it time.

By following this recipe, you can master the art of sending and receiving crypto, ensuring each transaction is as successful and stress-free as hosting a gathering of your closest friends and family.

Transferring significant funds, whether in the realm of cryptocurrency or traditional banking, can often feel like walking a tightrope without a safety net. The process can stir a cocktail of emotions, from the initial excitement and anticipation to anxiety and second-guessing. Managing these emotions is crucial, not only for your peace of mind but to ensure the transaction process is smooth and error-free. Think of it as performing on stage; the better you manage your nerves, the more likely you are to give a stellar performance.

Strategies for Managing Anxiety During Transactions

1. Preparation is Key: Just as a performer rehearses meticulously before the show, ensure you've prepared for your transaction. This means double-checking wallet addresses, ensuring you have enough funds, including transaction fees, and understanding the steps involved in sending or receiving crypto. Preparation can significantly reduce anxiety by providing a sense of control and readiness.

2. Verify Everything Before You Send: One of the main sources of stress in transferring funds is the fear of making a mistake. Like checking your equipment before a performance, verify all transaction details carefully. Ensure the recipient's address is correct by checking it multiple times and, if possible, confirm it through a direct communication channel with the recipient.

3. Understand Transaction Times: Just as different performances can vary in length, so can transaction confirmation times. Some transactions are confirmed within minutes, while others might take hours or, in extreme cases, days—especially during periods of high network congestion. Knowing this in advance can help set realistic expectations, much like knowing the duration of a play before you attend. If your transaction takes longer than anticipated, don't panic; it's likely just part of the process.

4. Trust the System's Design: The blockchain is designed with security in mind. It's a system that has undergone rigorous testing and continuous improvement. Reminding yourself of the inherent security features and the successful transactions that happen millions of times a day can be comforting. Think of it as trusting the safety features of a roller coaster; understanding the design and safety checks can ease the fear of the ride.

5. Step Away if Needed: If you've done everything right and the transaction is underway, take a break from the screen. Constantly checking for a confirmation can increase anxiety. Instead, engage in an activity that relaxes you or takes your mind off the transaction for a while. It's like taking a moment in the green room before going on stage; sometimes, a brief respite can help calm your nerves.

6. Use Support Networks: Just as performers have stagehands and fellow actors for support, don't hesitate to reach out to the community or support services if you have concerns or need reassurance about a transaction. Sometimes, just talking about your concerns can alleviate stress.

7. Reflect and Learn: After the transaction is complete, take some time to reflect on the process. Consider what went well and what could be improved next time. This reflection is akin to reviewing a performance; it's an opportunity to learn and grow, reducing anxiety for future transactions.

Managing the emotional aspects of transferring significant funds in cryptocurrency requires a balance of preparation, patience, and perspective. By adopting these strategies, you can navigate the process with a calmer, more composed mindset, ensuring that each transaction is handled with care and confidence, much like a seasoned performer taking the stage.

Chapter 3

Stoner's Guide to Market Analysis

Embarking on the journey of technical analysis in the cryptocurrency world can feel akin to learning the language of the universe, where each chart and graph holds the secrets to future market movements. At its core, technical analysis is the art of reading the market's tea leaves, gleaning insights from the patterns and rhythms of past price actions and trading volumes to predict where the wind might blow next.

Imagine you're chilling on your porch, watching the clouds roll by. You start to notice patterns—some clouds signal clear skies ahead, while others forewarn of a storm brewing. Technical analysis works much like this casual cloud-watching, except the clouds are historical data points on a price chart, and the weather forecast is your prediction for future price movements.

The Essence of Technical Analysis

At the heart of technical analysis is the belief that history tends to repeat itself. The market, in its vast complexity, moves in patterns that, once recognized, can offer insights into future movements. Think of your favorite album on vinyl; the needle follows the grooves, and though each track has its unique rhythm, the needle's path is predictable. Similarly, price movements in the crypto market follow 'grooves' that analysts try to decipher.

The Role of Price and Volume

Price: The price of a cryptocurrency is its immediate reflection, the culmination of all market actions and sentiments at any given moment. Tracking the price over time allows analysts to spot trends, much like identifying the crescendo in a symphony that hints at the climax to come.

Volume: Volume, or the number of coins traded within a certain period, acts as the chorus to the price's lead vocals. It provides a depth to the analysis, offering clues about the strength behind a price movement. High volume during a price increase suggests strong buying interest, akin to a crowd's roaring approval at a concert, affirming the performance's energy.

Charts and Patterns: The Visual Symphony

The visual representation of this data comes through charts, the stage upon which the drama of the market unfolds. Candlestick charts, line graphs, and bar charts transform dry numbers into a visual symphony, with each candle or line like a note contributing to the overarching melody. Analysts become conductors, interpreting the music and predicting its next movements.

Why It Matters

For the laid-back investor, mastering technical analysis is about more than just predicting the future; it's about understanding the market's language and feeling its pulse. It's a tool to navigate the crypto seas with a map that, while not predicting every wave, highlights the currents and the winds that could propel your journey forward.

As we delve deeper into the nuances of technical analysis, remember that it's not about having a crystal ball but about equipping yourself with a compass. With practice, patience, and a bit of intuition, you'll learn to read the market's signs as easily as watching the clouds on a lazy afternoon, making informed decisions that sail you smoothly through the volatile waters of the cryptocurrency market.

Diving into the world of cryptocurrency without understanding how to read crypto price charts is like hitting the surf without checking the surf report first. You might catch some waves, but you're also likely to wipe out more than you ride. Charts are the surf reports of the crypto world, offering a glimpse into the market's mood and movements. Let's break down the essentials: candlestick charts, volume bars, and moving averages, making them as easy to understand as deciding when to paddle out.

Candlestick Charts: The Wave Patterns

Candlestick charts are the backbone of crypto charting, offering a visual snapshot of price movements within a specific timeframe. Each "candle" provides four crucial pieces of information: the opening price, the closing price, the highest price, and the lowest price during that period, much like understanding the tide's high and low, the wave's crest and trough.

Body: The candle's thick part shows the opening and closing prices. A candle "fills" if it closes lower than it opens (usually red or black), indicating a price drop, akin to a wave that crashes down. If the candle closes higher than it opens, it's "hollow" (often green or white), indicating a price rise, much like a wave building up.

Wicks: The lines extending from the candle's body represent the highest and lowest prices during the timeframe, similar to the spray from the wave's crest or the depth beneath its trough. They show the price's reach beyond its open and close.

Volume Bars: The Ocean's Roar

Beneath the candlestick chart, you'll often find volume bars, each corresponding to a candle above. These bars indicate how many units of cryptocurrency were traded during that candle's timeframe. High volume bars, when paired with significant price movements, confirm the strength behind the move, much like the roar of the ocean confirming a wave's power. A big price move on thin volume might be less convincing, as a loud wave that fizzles out quickly.

Moving Averages: The Currents Below

Moving averages smooth out price data over a specified period to give a clear market trend direction, akin to understanding the underlying currents that influence wave patterns. They can be:

Short-term moving averages (like a 10-day MA) that follow the price closely, showing the immediate trend, much like spotting the immediate ripples and waves from the shore.

Long-term moving averages (like a 50-day or 200-day MA) that move slower and show the broader, underlying trend, similar to the deep currents that dictate the sea's overall movement.

When a short-term MA crosses above a long-term MA, it's often seen as a bullish signal, like spotting a strong current that suggests good waves ahead. Conversely, if the short-term MA crosses below, it might be time to be cautious, as the surf could be calming down.

Reading the Charts: Preparing to Surf

Just as a surfer uses the surf report to decide when to paddle out, a crypto investor uses these charting tools to make informed decisions about entering or exiting positions. Candlestick patterns can hint at future price movements, volume bars confirm the strength behind trends, and moving averages show the market's direction, helping you to catch the perfect wave or to sit one out until conditions improve.

By understanding these essentials, you're not just staring at lines and colors; you're interpreting the language of the crypto market. With practice, you'll learn to read these charts with the ease of a seasoned surfer scanning the horizon, ready to ride the big ones and avoid the wipeouts.

Identifying patterns on crypto charts is like recognizing shapes in nature, where certain formations can predict upcoming weather or the changing of seasons. In the realm of technical analysis, these patterns serve as indicators of potential market movements, offering insights into when to ride the wave or when to chill on the beach. Let's explore some basic chart patterns, comparing them to familiar sights in nature to make them more approachable.

Triangles: The Mountain Peaks and Valleys

Triangles on a chart can signal periods of consolidation before a breakout. They're akin to observing mountains and valleys, where the converging lines resemble the slopes leading up to a peak or descending into a valley. Triangles can be ascending, descending, or symmetrical, each telling a different story:

Ascending triangles, with a flat top and a rising bottom line, suggest that buyers are more aggressive than sellers, much like a mountain slope that steadily rises, hinting at the eventual breakthrough to the peak.

Descending triangles, with a flat bottom and a downward-sloping top line, indicate sellers pushing the price down against a level of support, similar to a valley floor that remains constant as the surrounding slopes decline.

Symmetrical triangles, where both the top and bottom lines converge towards each other, show a period of uncertainty, like a path through a dense forest where the way forward isn't clear until you emerge on the other side.

Head and Shoulders: The Rolling Hills

The head and shoulders pattern, comprising three peaks with the middle one standing out the tallest, mirrors the rolling hills on a landscape, where the central hill overshadows its neighbors. This formation often signals a reversal in trend:

In an uptrend, the appearance of a head and shoulders top can indicate that the price is set to decline, much like reaching the summit of a hill and preparing for the descent.

Conversely, an inverse head and shoulders pattern during a downtrend suggests a potential upward breakout, akin to coming out of a valley onto rising ground.

Double Tops and Bottoms: The Reflection in a Lake

Double tops and bottoms are patterns that signify a strong resistance level (double top) or support level (double bottom), reminiscent of seeing a mountain's peak or a valley's trough reflected perfectly in a lake's surface.

A double top looks like two adjacent peaks with a slight dip in the middle, indicating that the price attempted to break through a high point twice and might soon reverse downward, as if the peak is too steep to climb again.

A double bottom appears as two low points with a rise in between, signaling a potential upward reversal, much like finding a valley floor that you can ascend from, having gathered strength at its base.

Understanding these patterns is like becoming fluent in the language of the landscapes, allowing you to anticipate what might come next in the market's terrain. Just as a hiker learns to read the signs of the trail or a sailor the sea's moods, a crypto investor can use these natural analogies to navigate the market's highs and lows with greater confidence and intuition.

Navigating the ever-changing tides of the cryptocurrency market can feel like setting sail on the open sea. To steer through these waters, traders use technical indicators as navigational aids, helping to decipher when to catch the wave and when it's wiser to anchor down and wait. Among these tools, the Relative Strength Index (RSI) and the Moving Average Convergence Divergence (MACD) stand out for their utility in reading the market's currents. Let's explore these indicators in terms of natural analogies, making their functions both understandable and relatable.

Relative Strength Index (RSI): The Tide's Pull

Imagine you're at the beach, watching the waves. The tide's pull gives each wave its strength and direction, much like the RSI measures the velocity and magnitude of price movements. The RSI oscillates between 0 and 100, serving as a gauge for whether the market is considered overbought or oversold.

Overbought Conditions: When the RSI climbs above 70, it suggests that the market might be overextended, like a wave that's grown too tall and is ready to break. It's a signal that the tide may soon turn, and a downturn could be on the horizon.

Oversold Conditions: Conversely, if the RSI dips below 30, it indicates that the market may be undervalued, akin to the water pulling back, revealing the sand beneath. This can be a sign that an upward surge, or swell, is likely to follow.

Using the RSI, traders can feel the market's pulse, understanding when it's energized and ready to move, or when it's pulled back, ready for a push forward.

Moving Average Convergence Divergence (MACD): The Wind's Direction

The MACD is like reading the wind before setting sail. It consists of two moving averages (the MACD line and the signal line) and a histogram that measures the distance between them. This indicator helps traders identify the market's momentum, trend direction, and potential turning points.

Trend Direction: When the MACD line crosses above the signal line, it's akin to a favorable wind catching the sails, suggesting it's a good time to embark on your trade. This bullish crossover indicates that the market's momentum is picking up.

Trend Reversals: If the MACD line crosses below the signal line, it's as though the wind has shifted against you, suggesting a potential downturn or bearish movement. It might be a sign to hold off on trades until the winds are more favorable.

Momentum and Strength: The histogram provides insight into the strength of the trend. A widening histogram suggests increasing momentum, much like a strong wind propelling your boat forward, while a narrowing histogram signals that the trend might be losing strength, indicating calmer waters ahead.

Together, the RSI and MACD serve as essential tools in a trader's navigational kit, offering insights into the market's ebb and flow. Just as a sailor uses the tide and wind to decide when to set out and when to stay in port, crypto traders use these indicators to determine the optimal moments to enter or exit trades. By mastering these tools, traders can ride the market waves with confidence, knowing when to catch a ride on the bullish swells and when to wait for the bearish tides to turn.

Fundamental analysis in the realm of cryptocurrency is akin to the meticulous preparation and assessment of your gear before embarking on a long, immersive session in your favorite pursuit, be it a marathon gaming night, a deep dive into a creative project, or gearing up for a full day of surfing. Just as you wouldn't start without ensuring your equipment is top-notch and suited to the task ahead, fundamental analysis involves a thorough evaluation of all available information about a cryptocurrency to determine its underlying value.

Understanding the Core of Fundamental Analysis

At its heart, fundamental analysis is about getting to the essence of a cryptocurrency's intrinsic value, looking beyond the fluctuations of daily trading volumes and price swings. It's the equivalent of examining the craftsmanship of a surfboard, the specifications of a gaming console, or the quality of paint and brushes for an artist. This method scrutinizes various factors, including but not limited to:

Technology: Assessing the blockchain technology behind a cryptocurrency, its utility, scalability, and security features is like checking the tech specs of a piece of equipment. The goal is to understand whether it stands out for its innovation and functionality or if it's just another run-of-the-mill product.

Development Team: Just as you'd consider the reputation and track record of a gear manufacturer, analyzing the team behind a cryptocurrency project is crucial. Their expertise, commitment, and vision can significantly impact the project's success and, consequently, its value.

Market Position: Understanding a cryptocurrency's market position involves looking at its current use cases, adoption rate, and potential for growth. It's akin to evaluating whether a particular gear is a must-have in its field or if it's struggling to find its niche.

Regulatory Environment: The legal and regulatory landscape can greatly affect a cryptocurrency's potential for widespread adoption and stability. This analysis is like considering the legal restrictions and safety standards for equipment, which can either enhance its usability and acceptance or pose barriers.

Community and Ecosystem: The strength and engagement of the project's community can be a strong indicator of its health and potential for growth. Much like how robust community support can lead to better updates, mods, or uses for equipment, a vibrant cryptocurrency community can drive innovation and adoption.

Applying Fundamental Analysis

Fundamental analysis is about digging deep, gathering all this information, and piecing it together to form a comprehensive picture of a cryptocurrency's true worth. It requires a critical eye and the ability to sift through a lot of data, much like researching the best components for a custom-built PC or the ideal materials for a piece of art.

This approach enables investors to make informed decisions based on the project's long-term prospects rather than speculative short-term price movements. It's about betting on the quality and potential of the gear (in this case, the cryptocurrency) to perform over time, ensuring that you're well-equipped for the journey ahead in the digital currency landscape.

When venturing into the world of cryptocurrency through the lens of fundamental analysis, paying attention to key indicators and metrics is like selecting the finest ingredients for the ultimate munchie mix. Each element plays a crucial role in the final outcome, determining whether you'll end up with a satisfying snack or a bland, forgettable nibble. Let's explore these essential indicators, drawing parallels to culinary choices that resonate with the art of creating the perfect munchies.

Market Cap: The Main Ingredient

The market capitalization of a cryptocurrency is akin to the base ingredient of your munchies, such as the premium chocolate in a gourmet trail mix. Market cap—a calculation of the total value of all coins in circulation multiplied by the current price—gives you a sense of the cryptocurrency's overall market size and standing. A high market cap indicates a significant presence in the market, much like how using high-quality chocolate can elevate your snack mix, suggesting a more widely accepted and potentially stable investment.

Volume: The Spice Level

Trading volume represents the amount of the cryptocurrency that has been traded within a specific time frame, similar to the amount of spice or seasoning you decide to add to your dish. High volume indicates a lot of interest and activity, suggesting that the market is vibrant and liquid. Just as the right amount of seasoning can make a dish pop, adequate trading volume can signal a healthy, dynamic market for a cryptocurrency, making it easier to buy or sell without drastically affecting the price.

Technology and Innovation: The Unique Flavors

The underlying technology and innovation of a cryptocurrency project are comparable to the unique flavors that set your munchies apart. This could be the inclusion of exotic fruits or nuts that turn a simple trail mix into an extraordinary snack. In the crypto space, innovative features such as smart contracts, scalability solutions, or consensus mechanisms can set a project apart, offering unique value propositions that could drive future adoption and growth. Just as unique ingredients can create a memorable munchie mix, cutting-edge technology can position a cryptocurrency for long-term success.

Development Team: The Chefs Behind the Scenes

The project's development team is like the skilled chefs behind your favorite gourmet dish. Their expertise, experience, and commitment can significantly influence the project's success. A team with a strong track record, clear vision, and active engagement with the community can inspire confidence, much like how knowing a dish was prepared by an acclaimed chef can assure you of its quality. The team's ability to innovate, solve problems, and drive the project forward is crucial, underscoring the importance of the people behind the technology.

Community and Ecosystem: The Dining Experience

Finally, the strength and engagement of the project's community and ecosystem can be likened to the dining experience surrounding a meal. A supportive and active community, with developers, users, and advocates, contributes to a project's vibrancy and resilience, much like how enjoying your munchies in good company enhances the overall experience. A cryptocurrency with a robust ecosystem of partnerships, applications, and users indicates a healthy, growing project, suggesting it may be a more appetizing choice for long-term investment.

Just as every ingredient matters in creating the perfect munchies, each of these indicators plays a vital role in the fundamental analysis of a cryptocurrency. By examining these aspects, investors can better assess the potential value and viability of a crypto asset, making informed decisions that align with their investment goals and appetite for risk.

Evaluating a cryptocurrency project's fundamentals is akin to scouting the perfect spot for a laid-back afternoon. Just as you'd consider the ambiance, accessibility, and amenities of your chill-out spot, assessing a project's whitepaper, roadmap, and community engagement gives you a holistic view of its potential. Let's navigate through these elements, highlighting how each contributes to making an informed decision, much like choosing the ideal locale for your leisure time.

The Whitepaper: The Invitation

A project's whitepaper is the invitation to the party. It outlines the project's vision, technology, use cases, and how it intends to address specific problems within the blockchain ecosystem. Reading a whitepaper is like reading the description of a potential hangout spot; it gives you a feel for the vibe they're going for, the crowd it attracts, and whether it aligns with your tastes. Key things to look out for include:

The Problem and Solution: Just as you'd choose a beach for relaxation or a café for its coffee, identify what issue the project aims to solve and how effectively its proposed solution seems to be.

Technical Details: Understanding the technology behind the project is like knowing the amenities of your hangout spot. It's not just about having a great view (concept) but also about comfortable seating and good music (scalability, security, and user experience).

The Roadmap: The Event Schedule

A project's roadmap serves as its event schedule, outlining past milestones and future goals. It's akin to checking what activities are available at your chosen spot and when. Does the afternoon include live music, or is there a scheduled quiet time for relaxation? Similarly, a roadmap gives you insight into the project's development pace, its ambition, and whether it's meeting its goals, which helps gauge the team's reliability and commitment.

Community Engagement: The Atmosphere

The project's community is the atmosphere of your chosen spot. A vibrant, engaged community suggests a welcoming and dynamic environment, much like a beach with friendly locals and interesting activities. Evaluate the community's size, activity level on social media, forums, and the project's GitHub (for development activity). A supportive and active community not only contributes to the project's resilience but also its ability to innovate and grow. It's the difference between a lively gathering and a deserted venue.

Additional Considerations:

Partnerships and Collaborations: Just as the best spots often have connections with local artists or food vendors, a project's partnerships can significantly enhance its value and credibility.

Regulatory Compliance: Knowing that your hangout spot is legally compliant and safe gives peace of mind, similar to understanding how a project navigates the complex world of blockchain regulations.

When scouting for the best cryptocurrency project to invest in, think of it as choosing your ideal spot for a laid-back afternoon. The whitepaper invites you to explore the project's vision, the roadmap shows what's planned for the future, and the community's engagement sets the overall atmosphere. By thoroughly researching these aspects, you're not just making an informed investment decision; you're finding a project that resonates with your interests and values, promising a fulfilling and enjoyable experience in the crypto space.

Navigating the world of cryptocurrency without an understanding of broader economic and industry trends is akin to planning your outdoor activities without considering the season's vibes. Just as you wouldn't wear shorts and flip-flops in the dead of winter or bring a snowboard to the beach in summer, aligning your crypto investments with the prevailing economic climate and industry trends is crucial for success. Let's explore how these broader forces can impact cryptocurrency values, drawing parallels to staying in tune with the larger rhythm of the seasons.

Economic Trends: The Weather Patterns

Economic trends act like the weather patterns that dictate the season's overall mood. Factors such as inflation rates, interest rates, economic growth figures, and geopolitical events can significantly influence investor sentiment and, consequently, the value of cryptocurrencies.

Inflation and Interest Rates: Just as a long, harsh winter can drive people indoors, seeking warmth, high inflation rates might push investors towards cryptocurrencies as a hedge against dwindling purchasing power. Conversely, high interest rates might pull investors towards safer, interest-bearing assets, much like cooler temperatures might encourage more indoor activities.

Economic Growth: A booming economy, full of optimism and growth, can be likened to the vibrant energy of spring. It might encourage more speculative investments in cryptocurrencies, driven by a general appetite for risk and innovation.

Geopolitical Events: Just as an unexpected storm can disrupt a perfectly planned picnic, geopolitical unrest or regulatory changes in major economies can cause sudden and significant fluctuations in cryptocurrency markets, necessitating a nimble and adaptive strategy.

Industry Trends: The Cultural Currents

Industry trends, on the other hand, are like the cultural currents that define each season's unique flavor. Technological advancements, regulatory shifts, and changes in consumer behavior within the blockchain and financial sectors can all play pivotal roles in shaping the value and adoption of cryptocurrencies.

Technological Breakthroughs: Innovations such as the development of more scalable blockchain solutions or enhanced privacy features can act like the first warm days of spring, breathing new life into the cryptocurrency market and driving up values.

Regulatory Climate: Just as the cultural vibe of a summer festival season can uplift spirits, a favorable regulatory environment can bolster investor confidence and cryptocurrency prices. Conversely, regulatory crackdowns can have a chilling effect, much like an unseasonably cold spell in autumn.

Adoption and Integration: The increasing integration of cryptocurrencies in everyday commerce and finance, from payment solutions to institutional investment products, reflects a broadening acceptance, similar to how certain trends become embedded in cultural norms with the changing seasons.

Understanding and adapting to these economic and industry trends is crucial for any crypto investor. It requires a blend of constant learning, observation, and the flexibility to adjust your strategy in response to the changing environment. Just as a seasoned gardener knows to plant seeds in sync with the seasons for the best harvest, a savvy investor recognizes the importance of aligning their moves with the broader economic and industry trends, ensuring they're always in tune with the market's larger rhythm.

Sentiment analysis in the context of cryptocurrency is akin to gauging the mood of a gathering, determining whether the vibe is electric with excitement or laid-back and relaxed. It's a tool that measures the collective attitude and feelings of market participants towards a particular cryptocurrency, providing insights that are not immediately visible through traditional technical or fundamental analysis. This method is like tuning into the playlist of a party from afar, letting you sense the energy without stepping inside.

The Pulse of the Market

At its core, sentiment analysis listens to the heartbeat of the market. It sifts through social media posts, news articles, forum discussions, and even the tone of market commentary to gauge public perception. Much like observing the body language and conversation volume in a room can give you a sense of the party's mood, sentiment analysis tools use natural language processing and other computational methods to quantify the market's emotional state.

Why Sentiment Matters

The collective mood can significantly impact market movements. Positive sentiment, marked by an upbeat and energetic mood, can drive prices up as more people buy into the optimism. This is similar to a lively party where the enthusiasm is contagious, encouraging everyone to join the dance floor. Conversely, a somber or anxious sentiment can lead to sell-offs, much like a mellow or tense gathering might see guests bowing out early.

Tuning Into the Market's Mood

Understanding market sentiment is about tuning into the subtle cues and underlying currents. It involves:

Monitoring Social Media and News: Just as a party's vibe can shift with the music or conversations, market sentiment can change rapidly with breaking news or viral social media trends. Tools that aggregate and analyze these sources can provide real-time snapshots of the market's mood.

Analyzing Volume and Tone: The volume of discussion and the tone (positive, neutral, negative) surrounding a cryptocurrency can offer clues about the market's direction. High volumes of positive chatter can be likened to a crowded room buzzing with excitement, suggesting a bullish sentiment.

Community Engagement: The level of engagement within a cryptocurrency's community, including developer updates and user activity, can also influence sentiment. A vibrant and active community reflects a party in full swing, signaling strong support for the cryptocurrency.

Sentiment Analysis as a Navigational Tool

Just as you might choose your evening's destination based on the type of atmosphere you're seeking, sentiment analysis can help investors navigate the crypto market. By understanding the prevailing mood, investors can make more informed decisions, aligning their strategies with the market's emotional tide. It's a way to catch the wave of optimism or to steer clear of impending downturns, leveraging the collective sentiment to guide your investment journey.

Incorporating sentiment analysis into your market strategy is like developing a keen sense for the energy of a room, allowing you to move in harmony with the crowd, whether it's to join the dance or to know when it's time to call it a night.

Just as a skillful DJ selects tunes to match and elevate the mood of a party, various tools and resources are available to help cryptocurrency traders and investors gauge the market sentiment, ensuring their strategies harmonize with the current vibes of the crypto world. Here are some of the key tools that act as the turntables and sound systems of sentiment analysis, each playing a vital role in tuning into the market's mood.

Social Media Monitoring Tools

Social media platforms like Twitter, Reddit, and Telegram are the bustling party rooms of the cryptocurrency community, where the chatter and buzz can provide real-time insights into market sentiment. Monitoring tools such as TweetDeck, Social Mention, and Reddit's cryptocurrency forums help sift through the noise to identify trends, measure the volume of discussion, and analyze the tone of conversations about specific cryptocurrencies. These tools are like having an ear to the ground at a party, picking up on the most talked-about topics and the crowd's general mood.

Opinion Polls and Surveys

Opinion polls and surveys serve as direct feedback mechanisms, much like a DJ taking requests to gauge what the audience wants to hear next. Platforms like Telegram polls or crypto-specific survey sites allow the community to voice their opinions and predictions regarding market movements, upcoming ICOs, or sentiment towards specific projects. This direct input can be invaluable, akin to understanding the crowd's preferences, ensuring the music keeps everyone on the dance floor engaged.

Analytical Platforms and Aggregators

Several platforms aggregate data from various sources to provide a comprehensive view of market sentiment. Tools like The TIE, LunarCRUSH, and Santiment analyze social media posts, news articles, and trading data to offer sentiment scores and other metrics that indicate the market's current state. Think of these platforms as the DJ's soundboard, where inputs from multiple sources are mixed and balanced to create the perfect set that resonates with the audience.

Trading and Charting Platforms

Many trading platforms now incorporate sentiment analysis features directly into their charting software. By integrating sentiment indicators alongside traditional technical analysis tools, traders can see how sentiment trends correlate with price movements. This is similar to a DJ using beatmatching software to seamlessly blend tracks based on the tempo and energy of the music, ensuring a smooth flow that keeps the party alive.

Market News and Analysis Websites

Staying informed with the latest cryptocurrency news and market analysis is crucial for understanding the broader context influencing sentiment. Websites like CoinDesk, Cointelegraph, and CryptoSlate offer timely updates and expert opinions that can impact market perception. It's akin to a DJ staying updated with the latest hits and underground tracks, ensuring their playlist is fresh and in tune with the audience's tastes.

Employing these tools for sentiment analysis allows investors to align their strategies with the market's prevailing mood, capitalizing on bullish enthusiasm or exercising caution during bearish trends. Just as a DJ reads the room and adjusts their playlist to maintain the vibe, savvy investors use sentiment analysis tools to navigate the crypto market's ebbs and flows, ensuring their decisions resonate with the current sentiment and contribute to a successful investment journey.

Blending sentiment analysis with technical and fundamental analysis in cryptocurrency trading is akin to creating a harmonious mixtape that balances the beats of logic with the melodies of emotion. It's about achieving a holistic understanding of the market, where the hard facts meet the collective mood, allowing for decisions that are both informed and intuitive. Let's explore how to integrate these diverse strands of market analysis to navigate the crypto space with a more nuanced approach.

The Harmony Between Technical Analysis and Sentiment

Technical analysis, with its charts, patterns, and indicators, serves as the backbone of market analysis, providing a structured approach to predicting future price movements based on past performance. However, like a tracklist that needs a vibe to truly resonate with its audience, technical analysis alone may not capture the market's full spectrum. This is where sentiment analysis steps in, adding depth and context by measuring the market's emotional pulse.

Integrating sentiment data with technical analysis involves looking for confirmation or divergence between the two. For instance, if technical indicators suggest an uptrend but sentiment analysis reveals a growing unease or skepticism among investors, it may signal a potential reversal or a less robust trend than the technicals alone would indicate. This approach is like fine-tuning a playlist, ensuring the music not only matches the beat but also the mood of the room.

The Grounding Effect of Fundamental Analysis

While technical and sentiment analyses provide insights into market trends and emotions, fundamental analysis offers a grounding perspective based on the intrinsic value of a cryptocurrency. Evaluating a project's technology, team, market position, and growth potential is akin to choosing songs based on their musical quality and the artist's credibility, ensuring the playlist has substance beneath its style.

Incorporating fundamental analysis ensures that your investment decisions are rooted in the project's long-term viability rather than solely on market trends and sentiment. This can be particularly valuable in distinguishing between short-term hype and genuine, sustainable growth opportunities. It's about selecting tracks that have stood the test of time or show real promise, rather than those that are merely today's hits.

Achieving a Balanced Mix

To effectively blend these analyses, consider each method as a different instrument in an ensemble, with each contributing its unique sound to the overall performance. Start with the technical analysis to chart the market's direction and momentum. Layer in sentiment analysis to gauge investor enthusiasm or caution, adding texture and depth to your understanding. Finally, ground your strategy with fundamental analysis, ensuring the investments have a solid base in the project's real-world potential.

Regularly revisit and adjust your analysis mix, staying responsive to changes in market conditions and sentiment. Just as a DJ adjusts their set in real time to match the crowd's energy and feedback, a successful crypto investor remains adaptable, blending techniques to navigate the market's highs and lows.

Incorporating sentiment into your analysis isn't about following the crowd blindly but understanding its influence on the market dynamics. By balancing the facts with the feels, you ensure your investment decisions are not just a reflection of current trends but resonate with a deeper understanding of the market's rhythm and the projects' fundamental value.

Chapter 4

Crafting Your Trading Plan

Just as tuning into the right genre of music can set the mood for your day or night, understanding and choosing a trading style that harmonizes with your lifestyle and temperament can significantly influence your journey in the cryptocurrency market. Each trading style has its rhythm and pace, from the fast beats of day trading to the prolonged notes of position trading. Let's explore these various styles, helping you find the one that resonates with you, ensuring your trading experience is not just profitable but also enjoyable.

Day Trading: The Fast-Paced Mix

Day trading is the equivalent of a high-tempo electronic dance music set, where trades are opened and closed within the same day, capturing the market's immediate movements. This style suits those who prefer a fast-paced environment and are willing to dedicate the time to monitor the market closely throughout the day. It requires quick decision-making and a good grasp of technical analysis to make the most of short-term price fluctuations.

Pros: Potential for quick profits and no overnight market risk.

Cons: Requires constant market monitoring and can be highly stressful.

Swing Trading: The Groovy Playlist

Swing trading is like a playlist of groovy beats that you can enjoy over a few days or weeks. This style involves holding onto trades for several days or weeks to capitalize on anticipated upward or downward market movements. Swing traders ride the 'waves' of market trends, using a mix of technical and fundamental analysis to guide their decisions.

Pros: Doesn't require constant market monitoring; suits those with a patient outlook.

Cons: Holding positions overnight or longer can expose you to overnight market risk.

Position Trading: The Classic Album

Position trading is akin to sitting back and appreciating a classic album in its entirety, where trades can be held for months or even years. This style is based on the belief that long-term trends will result in significant profits, with less regard for short-term market fluctuations. Position traders use a deep understanding of fundamental analysis to pick their spots, much like choosing a timeless record that never gets old.

Pros: Minimal time commitment needed for market monitoring; potential for significant long-term profits.

Cons: Requires a large initial capital; profits realized in the long term.

Scalping: The Quick Beats

Scalping is the trading equivalent of flipping through songs, seeking quick hits. Scalpers aim to profit from very short-term market inefficiencies, often holding trades for just minutes—or even seconds. This style demands a high level of attention and quick execution, making it suitable for those who thrive on immediate action.

Pros: Opportunities for numerous trades throughout the day; minimal exposure to long-term market risk.

Cons: Highly time-consuming and stressful; profits per trade are usually small.

Choosing the right trading style is about matching your trading activities with your personal life rhythm, much like how you'd select music to fit your current vibe. Whether you're drawn to the quick tempo of day trading or the enduring rhythms of position trading, the key is to choose a style that feels in tune with your lifestyle, allowing you to enjoy the process as much as the profits. By aligning your trading style with your temperament and daily routine, you set the stage for a more satisfying and sustainable trading experience.

Diving back into the world of technical analysis is like revisiting your favorite tracks, discovering new layers and beats that you hadn't noticed before. Technical analysis tools are the instruments that help you fine-tune your trading strategy, enabling you to hit the right notes at the right time, whether you're in for a quick jam or a long composition. Let's do a brief encore of these tools, highlighting how they can harmonize with your trading style to identify entry and exit points, set stop-loss orders, and leverage indicators for more informed decisions.

Identifying Entry and Exit Points

Support and Resistance Levels: Imagine these as the floor and ceiling of a room where the price moves. Support levels are like a trampoline, where prices tend to bounce up, while resistance levels are akin to a ceiling that prices struggle to break through. Identifying these levels can help you find the right moments to enter (near support) or exit (near resistance) a trade.

Trend Lines: Drawing trend lines on charts is like sketching the trajectory of a melody. By connecting the highs and lows, you can visualize the market's direction—upward, downward, or sideways. Entering a trade in the direction of the trend can often lead to more harmonious outcomes.

Setting Stop-Loss Orders

Stop-Loss Orders: Think of stop-loss orders as your safety net, protecting you from falling too hard if a trade doesn't go as planned. Setting a stop-loss order means you're specifying the maximum amount you're willing to lose on a trade. It's like deciding beforehand how late you'll stay at the party, ensuring things don't go overboard.

Leveraging Indicators for Informed Decisions

Moving Averages (MAs): Moving averages smooth out price data over a specific period, providing a clearer view of the trend. Using MAs can help you identify the market's momentum and potentially signal when to enter or exit a trade. It's like using the rhythm of a song to find the perfect moment to jump in and dance.

Relative Strength Index (RSI): The RSI is a momentum oscillator that measures the speed and change of price movements, indicating overbought or oversold conditions. An overbought signal might suggest it's time to consider exiting, while an oversold condition could be your cue to enter. It's akin to reading the room's energy to decide when to amp up the vibe or when to mellow out.

Moving Average Convergence Divergence (MACD): The MACD identifies changes in momentum by comparing two moving averages, offering signals for potential reversals. This can be particularly useful to time your entries and exits, much like catching the wave of the beat at just the right moment.

No matter your trading style, these technical analysis tools can help guide your decisions, ensuring you're not trading based on a hunch but rather on a well-composed strategy. Whether you're making quick moves like a day trader or settling in for the long haul like a position trader, integrating these tools into your approach can help you navigate the market's ups and downs with greater confidence. Think of it as fine-tuning your playlist to suit the occasion, ensuring every trade fits the moment just right.

Navigating the tumultuous waves of the cryptocurrency market requires more than just analytical skills and knowledge; it demands a certain tranquility of mind, akin to finding your zen in the midst of a storm. Maintaining a level head amid market volatility is crucial for making informed decisions without succumbing to the emotional whirlpools of fear and greed. Let's explore strategies and mindfulness techniques specifically tailored for traders to keep the vibe mellow, even when the market gets choppy.

Establishing a Daily Mindfulness Routine

Begin each trading day with a mindfulness or meditation session to center yourself. This practice can be likened to tuning an instrument before a performance, ensuring you're in harmony with yourself and ready to face the market's fluctuations with clarity and composure. A simple routine can involve focusing on your breath, observing your thoughts without attachment, and setting a calm, focused intention for the day ahead.

The Art of Detached Observation

Practice detached observation of the market and your reactions to it. Imagine you're sitting by a river, watching leaves (market events) float by without feeling the need to catch or chase after them. This technique helps cultivate an emotional distance, enabling you to view market movements objectively, without being swayed by the tide of collective sentiment.

Embracing the Present Moment

Traders often find themselves either regretting past decisions or worrying about future outcomes, which can cloud judgment and lead to reactive decision-making. Embrace the present moment, focusing on the here and now. This approach is about appreciating the current state of the market as it is, much like enjoying a song for its melody and rhythm without worrying about how it began or how it will end.

Mindful Breathing During Volatility

When the market becomes particularly volatile, and emotions run high, turn to mindful breathing to regain your calm. Deep, slow breaths can act as an anchor, bringing you back to a state of equilibrium. It's akin to finding a quiet spot at a bustling party, allowing you a moment of peace amid the chaos.

Gratitude Practice

Incorporate a daily practice of gratitude into your trading routine. Reflect on what you're thankful for, including the learning opportunities the market provides, regardless of whether a trade was profitable. This practice can change your perspective, shifting focus from what was lost to the growth and knowledge gained. It's about enjoying the dance, regardless of the steps.

Setting Mindful Trading Reminders

Use reminders to maintain mindfulness throughout your trading day. These can be alarms or notes with messages that encourage you to take a moment, breathe, and reassess your state of mind. It's like having a playlist set up to remind you to change the tune if the energy starts to dip, ensuring the party stays lively and enjoyable.

Mindful Decompression Post-Trading

After the trading day ends, engage in activities that allow you to decompress and detach from the market. Whether it's yoga, a walk in nature, or listening to your favorite music, find what brings you back to a state of calm and contentment, readying you for the next day.

Integrating these mindfulness and meditation techniques into your trading routine can significantly enhance your emotional resilience, allowing you to navigate the highs and lows of the market with grace and stability. By maintaining a zen-like approach to trading, you ensure that the journey remains fulfilling and balanced, keeping the vibe mellow even in the face of the market's inevitable storms.

In the symphony of trading, setting stop-loss and take-profit points is akin to composing a piece with both highs and lows, ensuring that the music flows harmoniously without any discordant notes. These tools are essential for managing risk and protecting profits, allowing you to step away from the constant market monitoring and enjoy the other melodies of life. Let's explore how to use these tools effectively, ensuring your trading strategy plays out smoothly, even when you're not watching.

Stop-Loss Points: Your Safety Chords

A stop-loss order is like a safety chord in your trading melody. It automatically closes out a trade at a predetermined price level to prevent further losses if the market moves against you. Setting a stop-loss is deciding in advance the maximum amount of risk you're comfortable with, much like determining how loud you want a particular section of music to be before it becomes too overwhelming.

Determining Stop-Loss Levels: To set an effective stop-loss, consider the volatility of the cryptocurrency you're trading and your personal risk tolerance. A common method is to place it just below a recent support level for a buy order or above a recent resistance level for a sell order, allowing some room for natural market fluctuations.

Percentage-Based Stop-Loss: Another approach is to set your stop-loss at a certain percentage away from your entry point, ensuring that your losses never exceed a predetermined portion of your investment, much like setting volume limits on your speakers to prevent them from blowing out.

Take-Profit Points: Capturing the High Notes

Take-profit orders are the high notes in your trading composition, the moments you've been building up to. They automatically close your trade when the price reaches a certain level of profit, ensuring you capture your gains before the market sentiment changes. Setting take-profit points is like scripting the climax of a song, deciding how it will peak before gently bringing the listener back down.

Identifying Take-Profit Levels: These can be set at key resistance levels, previous highs, or using a risk-reward ratio that aligns with your trading strategy. For instance, if your stop-loss is set to a 5% loss, you might set your take-profit at a 15% gain, maintaining a 3:1 risk-reward ratio.

Trailing Stop-Loss: To maximize profits, consider using a trailing stop-loss, which adjusts your stop-loss level as the price moves in your favor. It's like improvising the end of your piece based on the audience's reaction, ensuring the final note resonates perfectly with the overall performance.

Balancing Act: Harmony Between Stop-Loss and Take-Profit

Finding the right balance between stop-loss and take-profit points is crucial. They must be set far enough from the entry point to allow the market to "breathe" and avoid getting stopped out by normal volatility, yet close enough to protect gains and limit losses effectively. It's the art of balancing the crescendos and decrescendos in your trading strategy, ensuring neither overshadows the other.

The Result: A Well-Composed Trading Strategy

By effectively setting stop-loss and take-profit orders, you compose a trading strategy that plays out as intended, whether you're actively watching the markets or enjoying your life's other pursuits. This approach allows you to engage in trading as part of a balanced lifestyle, ensuring that your involvement in the crypto market adds to your life's melody rather than detracting from it.

With these tools in place, you can step away from the constant market monitoring, confident that your trades will execute at the right moments, allowing you to savor the sweet sounds of success without missing a beat in the symphony of your daily life.

Portfolio diversification in the world of trading is much like creating the perfect playlist for an extended road trip. Just as you wouldn't want to listen to the same song on repeat, diversifying your investments ensures you're not overly exposed to the performance of a single asset. This strategy is about mixing different genres — or in this case, asset classes and cryptocurrencies — to create a harmonious balance that can weather various market conditions, minimizing risk while still offering the potential for rewarding returns.

Understanding Diversification

Diversification is the investment equivalent of spreading your interests across a wide range of activities. It involves allocating investments among various financial instruments, industries, and other categories to minimize the impact of any single asset's poor performance on the overall portfolio. The goal is to reduce the volatility of your portfolio over time, much like balancing energetic tracks with mellow tunes to create a more enjoyable listening experience.

Diversifying Across Cryptocurrencies

Cryptocurrency markets are known for their volatility, with prices swinging dramatically in short periods. Diversifying your crypto investments can help manage these risks:

Spread Across Categories: Consider investing across different categories of digital assets, such as Bitcoin, altcoins (like Ethereum, Litecoin), and tokens from various sectors (DeFi, gaming, NFTs). It's akin to mixing classic rock, indie, electronic, and other genres in your playlist.

Market Cap Consideration: Balance your portfolio with a mix of large-cap, mid-cap, and small-cap cryptocurrencies. Large-cap cryptos, like Bitcoin and Ethereum, are like the classic hits — generally more stable. In contrast, smaller caps can be the hidden indie gems with the potential for significant growth but higher volatility.

Diversifying Beyond Cryptocurrencies

While cryptocurrencies can offer high returns, they also come with high risks. Diversifying your investment portfolio beyond digital currencies can provide a buffer against crypto market volatility:

Traditional Stocks: Incorporating stocks into your portfolio adds a layer of stability, as they're influenced by different factors than cryptocurrencies. It's like adding well-known classics to your playlist that you know will always be hits.

Bonds and Fixed Income: Bonds offer a fixed return over time and can serve as the slow, steady tracks that ensure your portfolio has a calm base.

Real Estate and Commodities: Real estate and commodities like gold can hedge against inflation, adding another layer of diversification. These are your timeless tracks, likely to hold their value over time.

Achieving Harmony Through Diversification

Effective diversification requires more than just owning different assets; it's about finding the right balance that aligns with your risk tolerance and investment goals. Regularly review and adjust your portfolio composition to ensure it remains well-diversified in response to changing market dynamics and personal goals, much like updating your playlist to keep it fresh and relevant.

The Takeaway

Diversification is a key strategy for managing investment risk and aiming for more stable returns. By spreading your investments across a variety of asset classes and within the cryptocurrency space, you can create a resilient portfolio that's capable of weathering market ups and downs — all while enjoying the journey, confident in the knowledge that you've set up your investment playlist to suit any market mood or moment.

In the fast-paced world of cryptocurrency trading, where fortunes can seemingly be made or lost in the blink of an eye, the allure of quick wins can be irresistible. Yet, it's the traders who embrace a patient, long-term approach that often find themselves on the path to sustainable success. Much like the greatest albums that need time to be appreciated fully, a thoughtful investment strategy unfolds its true potential over time. Let's explore the benefits of adopting a slow and steady approach to trading, highlighting real-life success stories of those who thrived by staying cool, collected, and focused on the long game.

The Virtues of Patience in Trading

Patience in trading is akin to cultivating a garden; it's about planting seeds, nurturing them, and understanding that growth takes time. In the volatile landscape of cryptocurrencies, a long-term outlook helps investors:

Mitigate Risk: By not reacting to short-term market fluctuations, long-term traders can avoid making impulsive decisions based on temporary emotions or events.

Capitalize on Compound Growth: Just as a well-tended garden yields more produce over time, a long-term investment strategy allows for the compounding of gains, where profits generate more profits.

Benefit from Market Cycles: Understanding that markets move in cycles allows long-term traders to weather downturns with the confidence that uptrends will eventually return, much like seasonal changes in a garden.

Real-Life Success Stories

Satoshi Nakamoto's Vision

While not a trader per se, the mysterious creator of Bitcoin, Satoshi Nakamoto, embodies the ultimate long-term vision. Launching Bitcoin in 2009 with little fanfare, Satoshi's patience and foresight have paved the way for what has become a revolutionary asset class. Bitcoin's journey from a value of nearly zero to tens of thousands of dollars per coin is a testament to the power of a long-term, visionary approach in the face of skepticism and volatility.

The Early Bitcoin Investors

Consider the stories of early Bitcoin investors who, recognizing the potential of digital currencies, held onto their investments through various market cycles, including dramatic peaks and troughs. One notable example is Kristoffer Koch, who invested $27 in Bitcoin in 2009 and forgot about it. Rediscovering his investment years later, he found it was worth over $886,000. These investors, by holding their nerve and maintaining a long-term perspective, reaped significant rewards.

Ethereum's Co-Founder

Vitalik Buterin, co-founder of Ethereum, is another exemplar of long-term thinking in the crypto space. Despite the platform's early challenges and the volatile market, Buterin's steadfast belief in Ethereum's potential and his continuous work on improving the ecosystem have seen Ethereum grow to become the second-largest cryptocurrency by market cap. His approach underscores the value of patience and persistence in achieving lasting impact.

Embracing the Slow and Steady

Embracing a slow and steady approach to trading doesn't mean inaction. Instead, it involves:

Regular Market Analysis: Keeping abreast of market trends and technological developments to make informed adjustments to your investment strategy.

Disciplined Investment: Continually investing in a diversified portfolio, taking advantage of dollar-cost averaging to smooth out the volatility.

Personal Growth: Using the time to expand your knowledge of blockchain technology, market analysis techniques, and financial management.

By adopting a patient, long-term approach to trading, investors can navigate the tempestuous seas of the cryptocurrency market with a sense of calm and purpose. The success stories of those who have thrived by staying cool and collected serve as a powerful reminder that, in the world of investing, sometimes the best strategy is to tune out the noise, focus on the horizon, and let time work its magic.

In the world of cryptocurrency trading, where success stories and tales of sudden fortunes can dominate the conversation, it's essential to pause and reflect on what success truly means to you. Much like creating a personal playlist that resonates with your unique taste and experiences, defining success in trading should be a deeply personal endeavor, tailored to your values, life goals, and the rhythm of your daily life. This section encourages you to set personal benchmarks for success, emphasizing the importance of staying true to yourself amidst the external hype and peer pressure.

Tune Into Your Values

Success in trading, or in any endeavor, isn't a one-size-fits-all concept. It's more akin to selecting music for your playlist; what uplifts and motivates one person might not resonate with another. Begin by identifying your core values and what you're ultimately striving to achieve through trading. Is it financial independence, the thrill of the trade, contributing to innovative projects, or perhaps a blend of these? Aligning your trading goals with your broader life values ensures that your journey is fulfilling and true to your personal ethos.

Set Your Life Goals as Your North Star

Your life goals are the North Star guiding your trading journey. Just as a traveler uses the stars to navigate, let your life goals illuminate your path in the often chaotic and unpredictable crypto market. Whether it's securing your family's future, funding your passions, or creating a foundation for future ventures, these goals should frame your definition of success. Setting specific, measurable, achievable, relevant, and time-bound (SMART) goals can help translate these broader aspirations into actionable trading strategies.

Navigate Beyond the Hype

The crypto world is rife with stories of overnight millionaires and tales of catastrophic losses, creating a whirlwind of emotions and expectations for traders. It's crucial to navigate this noise with a sense of equanimity, much like finding peace in your favorite song amid a cacophony. Recognize that your trading journey is unique, and measure your progress against your personal benchmarks, not someone else's highlight reel. Embracing a mindset of continuous learning and growth, rather than chasing quick wins, can lead to more sustained and meaningful achievements.

Embrace Your Unique Trading Rhythm

Just as every music enthusiast has their unique taste, every trader has their rhythm that suits their lifestyle and risk tolerance. Some may thrive on the fast-paced trading of day trading, while others may find their groove in the slow, steady approach of position trading. Experiment with different styles, and be willing to adjust as you learn more about the market and yourself. Finding the trading rhythm that complements your life ensures that trading remains a source of joy and fulfillment, not a cause of undue stress.

Celebrate Personal Milestones

In the pursuit of your goals, remember to celebrate the milestones along the way. These celebrations are your personal accolades, acknowledging the effort, learning, and resilience you've shown on your journey. Whether it's successfully executing a complex trade, reaching a savings goal, or simply gaining a deeper understanding of the market, each milestone is a step towards your definition of success.

Defining success on your own terms in the world of cryptocurrency trading means crafting a journey that's in harmony with who you are and what you value most. By setting personal benchmarks for success, guided by your values and life goals, you can navigate the market with confidence and authenticity, ensuring that the path you tread is distinctly your own.

The concept of compounding in finance is akin to the art of building a meticulously curated playlist, where each addition enriches the collection, gradually transforming it into a vast treasury of tunes that soundtrack your life. In the realm of cryptocurrency trading, embracing the power of compounding involves recognizing how small, regular profits can accumulate over time, weaving a tapestry of wealth that, while not immediately apparent, becomes significant through patience and persistence.

Understanding Compounding

Compounding in trading is the process by which an investment grows over time as earnings from both the initial principal and the accumulated earnings from preceding periods contribute to the investment's growth. It's the financial equivalent of adding a song to your playlist and then discovering an entire genre that resonates with your soul, each track adding depth and diversity to your collection.

The Slow Build

Just as a great playlist isn't created overnight but is the result of many thoughtful additions over time, compounding wealth through trading requires a long-term perspective. The key is consistency and reinvestment of profits. Even modest returns, when consistently reinvested, can grow exponentially over time due to the compounding effect. It's like the joy of finding a new song or artist; the initial discovery is just the beginning, with the real growth in appreciation coming as you explore more deeply over time.

Practical Steps to Leverage Compounding

Regular Investment: Start by setting aside a consistent portion of your income for investment, much like dedicating time each week to discover new music. This regular investment habit ensures that you're continually contributing to your portfolio's growth.

Reinvesting Profits: Instead of cashing out your trading profits, consider reinvesting them into the market. Over time, these reinvested earnings will start to generate their own earnings, much like how one song leads you to another, gradually building a richer, more diverse collection.

Patience is Key: The true power of compounding is realized over the long term. The initial growth might seem slow, much like waiting for a playlist to take shape, but given time, the exponential nature of compounding takes effect, significantly amplifying your investment.

The Impact of Compounding

The impact of compounding on your trading portfolio can be profound. With each reinvestment, your capital base expands, enhancing your ability to generate earnings. This growth, over time, can lead to wealth far exceeding what might be achieved through simple linear growth. It's the difference between a playlist with a few cherished songs and a comprehensive collection that has a track for every mood and moment, lovingly curated over years.

Celebrating the Journey

Embracing the power of compounding in trading is as much about celebrating the journey as it is about the destination. Each reinvestment, each decision to let your profits build, is a step towards a future where your financial foundation is as robust and diverse as a well-crafted playlist. The key is to start early, remain consistent, and have the patience to let the magic of compounding work over time.

Understanding and leveraging the power of compounding allows traders to see beyond the immediate horizon, recognizing the potential for small, regular profits to accumulate into significant wealth. Much like how a carefully nurtured playlist becomes a soundtrack to your life, a disciplined approach to trading and reinvestment can weave a tapestry of financial security and abundance that supports your long-term goals and dreams.

Trading, much like any passionate endeavor, has the potential to consume your attention and energy, morphing from an engaging activity into an all-encompassing obsession. Balancing trading with the other facets of your life ensures that it adds value and excitement without detracting from your overall well-being and happiness. Just as a well-curated playlist blends seamlessly into the background of a gathering, enhancing the atmosphere without overpowering it, trading should enrich your life, not overwhelm it. Here are some tips to help maintain that balance, ensuring trading remains a harmonious part of a well-rounded lifestyle.

Set Defined Trading Hours

Just as you might allocate specific times for work, exercise, and leisure, establish clear boundaries for trading. Decide on the hours you will dedicate to market analysis, trading, and research, and stick to them. This structure helps prevent trading from bleeding into time reserved for family, friends, and relaxation, much like how a DJ sets boundaries to prevent a party from continuing indefinitely into the night.

Automate Where Possible

Utilize trading tools and platforms that offer automation options, such as setting stop-loss orders, take-profit levels, and even automated trading based on specific criteria. Automation can act as your playlist on shuffle, allowing you to enjoy the music without constantly manning the DJ booth. It reduces the need for continuous market monitoring, freeing you to focus on other activities while still engaging in trading.

Cultivate Interests Outside of Trading

Diversifying your interests ensures that your identity and happiness aren't solely tied to trading successes or failures. Engage in hobbies, exercise, social activities, and personal projects that bring you joy and relaxation. This diversification is akin to having a varied music collection, ensuring that if one genre starts to feel stale, you have others to turn to for refreshment and enjoyment.

Practice Mindfulness and Stress Reduction

Incorporate mindfulness practices into your daily routine to manage stress and maintain perspective. Activities such as meditation, yoga, and spending time in nature can help ground you, much like a calming track can soothe the soul after an upbeat dance set. These practices aid in keeping trading anxieties at bay and promote a sense of inner peace, regardless of market conditions.

Keep a Journal

Maintain a trading journal, but also consider keeping a personal journal to reflect on your experiences, challenges, and achievements both within and outside of trading. This reflection can provide insights into how trading is impacting your life and whether adjustments are needed to maintain balance. It's like reviewing a playlist after a party to understand which tracks uplifted the mood and which didn't quite fit.

Prioritize Health and Relationships

Never let trading compromise your health or relationships. Regular exercise, healthy eating, adequate sleep, and quality time with loved ones are foundational to a fulfilling life. These aspects are the bassline to your life's soundtrack, essential and unmissable. Ensure trading activities enhance these areas rather than detract from them.

Celebrate All Wins, Not Just Trading Ones

Acknowledge and celebrate achievements across all areas of your life, not just trading. Recognizing successes in personal development, relationships, and other hobbies reinforces the value of a balanced approach to life. It's about appreciating the entire concert, not just a single performance.

By implementing these strategies, you can ensure that trading remains a vibrant and rewarding part of your life's symphony, adding excitement and opportunity without overshadowing the melody of day-to-day living. Balancing trading with a rich tapestry of other activities and interests ensures a harmonious, fulfilling lifestyle, allowing you to enjoy the best of all worlds.

Chapter 5

The Munchies of Trading

Tools and Platforms

In the world of cryptocurrency trading, where the markets never sleep, and opportunities can arise at any moment, the importance of an intuitive interface cannot be overstated. Just as the perfect chill-out spot is easy to settle into, with everything you need within arm's reach, a trading platform should offer ease of use, enabling you to navigate its features and functionalities smoothly, even when your focus is more on the relaxed side. This section explores why an intuitive interface is crucial for traders seeking a laid-back yet effective trading experience.

The Comfort of Familiarity

An intuitive trading platform is like your favorite lounge chair — familiar, comfortable, and perfectly contoured to your preferences. It's about creating an environment where you feel in control and at ease, with tools and information laid out in a logical, accessible manner. This familiarity becomes especially important in a relaxed state of mind, where you want to minimize stress and confusion.

Streamlined Decision-Making

In the fast-paced crypto market, decision-making needs to be quick and informed. An intuitive interface supports this by ensuring that key information — such as asset prices, charting tools, and your portfolio performance — is presented clearly and accessibly. Think of it as having a well-organized record collection where you can find exactly what you want to play without any fuss, allowing you to enjoy the music (or in this case, trading) without unnecessary interruptions.

Reducing the Risk of Mistakes

When your focus is relaxed, the likelihood of making errors — whether it's clicking the wrong button or misreading a chart — increases. An intuitive, well-designed platform mitigates this risk by minimizing clutter and confusion, much like how a well-lit path at night reduces the chance of stumbling. Clear labels, logical navigation, and confirmation prompts for trades can act as guideposts, ensuring you stay on the right track even when you're in a mellow mood.

Customization and Personalization

A platform that allows for customization adds another layer of comfort and ease. Being able to personalize your dashboard, set up your own trading alerts, and organize information to suit your trading style makes the experience not only more intuitive but also more enjoyable. It's akin to tailoring a playlist for different moods or settings — the more personalized it is, the more it enhances your experience.

Accessibility Across Devices

Finally, the ease of use extends to accessibility across devices. Whether you prefer trading on a desktop, browsing on a tablet, or checking updates on your smartphone, the transition should be seamless. This flexibility ensures that you can engage with the trading platform wherever you are, in much the same way that streaming your favorite tunes on different devices keeps the vibe going wherever you roam.

Choosing a trading platform with an intuitive interface is about ensuring that your trading journey is as smooth and enjoyable as possible, enhancing your ability to engage with the market effectively, without the need for constant, high-strung focus. It's about making trading a harmonious part of your lifestyle, allowing you to stay chill while still capturing the opportunities that the ever-vibrant crypto market has to offer.

In the realm of cryptocurrency trading, where digital assets traverse the vast and sometimes shadowy expanse of the internet, robust security measures are the high walls and fortified gates that keep your treasure safe. Just as you'd invest in a sturdy lock for your front door or a reliable alarm system for your home, prioritizing security features in your trading platform is essential for safeguarding your investments and ensuring peace of mind. Let's delve into the significance of these security measures and how they serve as the guardians of your digital wealth.

The Foundation of Trust

Security is the bedrock upon which the trust between a trader and a platform is built. In an environment where digital assets can be highly attractive to cyber-thieves, a platform's commitment to security reflects its dedication to protecting its users. It's akin to choosing a bank for your savings; just as you'd select a financial institution known for its robust security protocols, opting for a trading platform with stringent security measures ensures your assets are in a safe vault, not a paper bag.

Essential Security Features

Two-Factor Authentication (2FA): This adds an extra layer of security by requiring two forms of identification before access is granted. It's like having a double lock on your door, where a key and a code are needed to enter.

Cold Storage: The equivalent of a high-security safe, cold storage refers to keeping a portion of the platform's assets offline, away from the reach of potential online attackers. This ensures that even in the event of a cyber breach, the majority of funds remain untouched.

Encryption: Strong encryption protocols act as the invisible, yet impenetrable, walls around your data. They ensure that even if information were intercepted, it would remain a jumbled, unreadable mess to the intruder.

Regular Security Audits: Ongoing security assessments by independent firms are akin to regular check-ups that assess the health and integrity of the platform's security infrastructure, ensuring that it remains fortified against new and emerging threats.

The Ripple Effect of Security Breaches

A security breach can have far-reaching consequences, eroding trust not only in the affected platform but in the cryptocurrency ecosystem as a whole. The impact of such breaches is twofold: there's the immediate financial loss for users whose assets are compromised, and there's the long-term damage to the reputation and reliability of the platform. It's a reminder that, in the digital realm, security is not just a feature but a necessity, much like airbags in a car or life jackets on a boat.

User Responsibility in Security

While trading platforms shoulder the responsibility of implementing robust security measures, users play a crucial role in safeguarding their assets. Practices such as using strong, unique passwords, being wary of phishing attempts, and keeping personal keys secure are the individual layers of armor that complement the platform's defenses.

Choosing a trading platform with top-notch security features offers more than just protection for your assets; it provides peace of mind, freeing you to focus on your trading strategy rather than worrying about the safety of your investments. In the unpredictable seas of cryptocurrency trading, security is the lighthouse guiding you safely to shore, ensuring that your journey is not only profitable but secure.

Navigating the diverse landscape of cryptocurrency trading platforms, each with its unique fee structure, can feel akin to exploring a vast marketplace, searching for the best deal on your favorite vinyl records. Just as the price tag and sound quality are critical factors in your purchase decision, understanding and comparing the fees and commissions associated with different trading platforms is essential to ensure you're getting the best value without compromising on quality. Let's break down the key components of fees and commissions, offering insights into how to evaluate these costs effectively.

Types of Fees on Trading Platforms

Trading Fees: These are charges applied to each trade you make, typically calculated as a percentage of the trade volume. Imagine this as the price of admission to an exclusive concert; the rate can vary significantly depending on the venue (platform) and the act (trade size and type).

Withdrawal and Deposit Fees: Some platforms charge fees for depositing or withdrawing funds from your account. It's similar to the service charges you might pay for using ATM machines outside your bank's network — an extra cost for accessing your money in certain ways.

Spread: The spread is the difference between the buying and selling price of an asset. It can be thought of as the markup on a collectible — the gap between what it costs the store and what you pay as the buyer.

Other Miscellaneous Fees: Be on the lookout for additional costs, such as inactivity fees or account maintenance charges, akin to the cleaning fee for a record player or the storage fee for your collection.

Comparing Platform Fees

To ensure you're getting the best deal, it's crucial to:

Read the Fine Print: Much like scrutinizing the condition and authenticity of a rare record, carefully review the fee structure detailed on the platform's website or user agreement.

Use Fee Calculators: Many platforms offer calculators to estimate your total costs based on your trading volume and frequency. This is akin to using a budgeting tool to plan your record purchases, ensuring you stay within your means.

Consider the Total Cost of Trading: The platform with the lowest trading fees isn't always the cheapest option. Sum up all potential costs, including withdrawal and deposit fees, to get a comprehensive view of what you'll be spending, similar to considering both the price of a record and the potential shipping costs.

Quality Over Cost

While finding a platform with competitive fees is important, it's equally crucial to weigh the cost against the quality of service offered. Consider factors such as security measures, user interface, customer support, and the range of available assets. A platform that charges slightly higher fees but offers superior security and user experience can be worth the extra cost, much like paying a premium for a collector's edition of your favorite album for its enhanced features and quality.

Regularly Review Your Options

The cryptocurrency market and its platforms are dynamic, with fee structures subject to change. Regularly reviewing your chosen platform and comparing it with others in the market ensures you continue to trade on terms that best suit your needs. It's like staying abreast of new releases and special editions in the music world — keeping your collection both up-to-date and meaningful.

Understanding and carefully selecting a trading platform based on its fees and commissions, balanced against the quality of service, empowers you to trade efficiently and cost-effectively. This approach ensures that your trading experience remains harmonious, allowing you to focus on the rhythm of the markets without getting sidelined by excessive costs.

The allure of cryptocurrency trading lies not just in the potential for profit but also in the rich diversity of assets available, offering a wide canvas for traders to express their strategies and preferences. Much like a gourmet chef relishes the availability of exotic ingredients to create masterful dishes, or a music enthusiast values a broad record collection that spans genres and eras, having access to a wide range of cryptocurrencies and other assets is crucial for traders seeking to diversify their portfolios and explore new opportunities. Let's delve into the significance of asset variety in trading platforms and how it caters to your diverse tastes and strategies.

The Spice of Trading: Asset Variety

Asset variety in trading platforms acts as the spice that flavors your trading experience. The ability to trade across a broad spectrum of cryptocurrencies, from well-established coins like Bitcoin and Ethereum to emerging altcoins and tokens, opens up a world of possibilities. This diversity allows traders to:

Diversify Risk: Just as a chef uses a mix of ingredients to balance flavors and create a more complex dish, traders can spread their risk across different assets. This diversification is crucial in the volatile crypto market, where the fortunes of one coin can sharply diverge from another.

Explore New Opportunities: A wide range of assets provides fertile ground for discovering undervalued coins with growth potential, akin to a music lover finding an obscure album that becomes a personal favorite. This exploration can uncover profitable trading opportunities before they become mainstream.

Adapt to Market Changes: The cryptocurrency market is dynamic, with new trends and sectors emerging regularly (e.g., DeFi, NFTs, Metaverse). A platform that offers a variety of assets allows traders to pivot their strategies and capitalize on these trends, much like a DJ adapts their playlist to the evolving tastes of their audience.

Choosing a Platform with Diverse Assets

When selecting a trading platform, consider not just the number of assets listed but also the diversity of those assets. Look for platforms that offer:

A Broad Selection of Cryptocurrencies: Platforms should list a wide range of coins, including major cryptocurrencies, altcoins, and tokens from various sectors, providing a broad field for investment and speculation.

Fiat Currency Options: The ability to trade against different fiat currencies (USD, EUR, GBP, etc.) can offer flexibility and hedging options against crypto volatility, much like having a versatile kitchen that can handle multiple cuisines.

Other Financial Instruments: Some platforms also offer derivatives, ETFs, or tokenized versions of traditional assets, adding another layer of diversity and strategy to your trading, akin to having both vinyl records and digital music at your disposal for different listening experiences.

Asset Variety as a Reflection of Your Trading Identity

Just as every chef has their signature dishes and every music enthusiast their preferred genres, your choice of assets reflects your unique trading identity. Whether you're drawn to the stability of major cryptocurrencies, the innovation within the DeFi space, or the speculative potential of new tokens, the variety of assets at your disposal allows you to craft a portfolio that truly resonates with your trading philosophy and goals.

In conclusion, the importance of asset variety in a trading platform cannot be overstated. It not only enriches your trading experience, offering avenues for diversification and exploration but also empowers you to craft a portfolio that mirrors your unique tastes and strategies. Just as a well-stocked kitchen inspires culinary creativity and a diverse record collection enriches your musical journey, access to a wide range of cryptocurrencies and assets fuels your trading adventure, opening up a world of possibilities.

The essence of a vibrant trading experience often extends beyond the charts and the thrill of a well-placed trade. Like the warmth felt from a tightly-knit community around a bonfire or the reassurance of expert advice during a challenging hike, the platform's community engagement and the quality of customer support play pivotal roles in enriching your trading journey. This section explores how to evaluate these aspects, ensuring you're not just choosing a platform but a supportive base camp for your trading adventures.

Community Engagement: The Collective Vibe

A platform's community is its heartbeat, pulsating with the shared excitement, concerns, and aspirations of its users. Engaging with this community can provide a wealth of knowledge, from trading strategies and market insights to updates and news. It's akin to joining a music festival crowd, where each participant adds to the collective experience, making it richer and more vibrant.

Forums and Discussion Boards: Check if the platform hosts active forums or discussion boards. These spaces allow you to connect with fellow traders, exchange ideas, and gain new perspectives, much like sharing stories and tips around a campfire.

Social Media Presence: A strong social media presence can indicate a platform's commitment to engaging with its user base. Platforms that regularly update their channels with informative content, interact with users, and foster a sense of community are akin to artists who engage with their fans, creating a more immersive experience.

Educational Resources: Platforms that offer tutorials, webinars, and educational resources contribute to the community's growth, empowering users with knowledge. It's like having an experienced guide who ensures everyone can navigate the trail confidently.

Quality of Customer Support: The Support Crew

In the unpredictable terrain of cryptocurrency trading, having a reliable support crew can make all the difference. Quality customer support ensures that, should you encounter an issue or need guidance, help is just a call or click away, providing a safety net that allows you to explore the market with confidence.

Availability and Accessibility: Evaluate the support team's availability. Platforms offering 24/7 support through multiple channels (live chat, email, phone) ensure that, much like a well-stocked first aid kit, help is readily available whenever you need it.

Response Time and Efficiency: Consider the average response time and the efficiency of resolving issues. A support team that quickly addresses and resolves queries is akin to having a responsive and knowledgeable crew ready to assist, ensuring minor issues don't turn into major setbacks.

Language Support: For a global user base, multilingual support can be crucial. It ensures that the platform is accessible to traders from various backgrounds, much like having a guide who speaks multiple languages, making everyone feel included and supported.

The Role of Community and Support in Your Trading Journey

Choosing a trading platform with vibrant community engagement and robust customer support is choosing a path lined with allies. The community offers a network of fellow travelers, ready to share their maps and experiences, while quality support acts as your compass, guiding you through foggy patches. Together, they create an environment where learning, growth, and exploration are not just encouraged but celebrated.

In conclusion, evaluating a platform's community engagement and the quality of customer support is about ensuring that your trading experience is supported by a robust infrastructure of knowledge, assistance, and camaraderie. It's about finding a place where you can thrive, surrounded by a community that cheers on your successes and a support team that's ready to assist when challenges arise, making your trading journey not just profitable but also profoundly rewarding.

In today's fast-paced world, where the lines between work, play, and rest often blur, the convenience of mobile trading apps has become a game-changer in the cryptocurrency space. Just as streaming services have transformed the way we listen to music, allowing us to enjoy our favorite tunes whether we're on a morning jog, cooking dinner, or chilling on the couch, mobile trading apps have revolutionized the trading experience. They offer the ultimate flexibility, enabling traders to stay connected to the markets from anywhere, at any time. Let's explore how these apps keep the trading process laid-back and accessible, blending seamlessly into your lifestyle.

Trade Anytime, Anywhere

The primary allure of mobile trading apps is their ability to untether you from the desktop, breaking down the walls of the traditional trading floor. Whether you're catching waves at the beach, hiking up a mountain, or lounging in your backyard, the market moves with you. This omnipresence ensures you never miss a beat, much like how your favorite playlist is always a few taps away, ready to set the mood or enhance the moment.

User-Friendly Interfaces

Designed with the user in mind, mobile trading apps often boast intuitive interfaces that simplify the complexity of trading. Navigating trades, analyzing charts, or checking your portfolio becomes as easy and enjoyable as scrolling through your social media feed or choosing the next song. This user-centric design ensures that, even for those new to trading or when your focus is more relaxed, the experience remains straightforward and stress-free.

Real-Time Alerts and Notifications

Staying informed is crucial in the volatile crypto market, and mobile apps excel by providing real-time alerts and notifications. Whether it's a significant price movement, a news update, or a reminder about your set orders, these notifications act like a personal assistant, keeping you in the loop without the need for constant monitoring. It's the equivalent of having a friend who alerts you when your favorite band drops a new album or when tickets go on sale, ensuring you never miss out.

Security at Your Fingertips

Despite their accessibility, mobile trading apps do not compromise on security. With features like biometric authentication (fingerprint or facial recognition), two-factor authentication, and secure encryption, these apps ensure that your digital assets and personal information are protected, offering peace of mind. It's akin to having a secure lock on your digital music library, safeguarding your collection from prying eyes.

A Gateway to Learning and Growth

For those looking to deepen their understanding of the cryptocurrency market, many mobile trading apps provide educational resources, market analyses, and demo trading accounts. This wealth of information is at your fingertips, ready to be explored at your leisure, much like how music streaming apps offer curated playlists and recommendations to discover new genres and artists.

The Symphony of Convenience

Mobile trading apps harmonize the convenience, accessibility, and security of trading into a symphony that resonates with the modern trader's lifestyle. They democratize access to the cryptocurrency markets, ensuring that anyone, regardless of their schedule or location, can participate in the financial revolution. Just as music streaming apps have become a staple for audiophiles, mobile trading apps are becoming indispensable for traders who value freedom, flexibility, and the ability to stay connected to the pulse of the market, all while keeping the process as laid-back and enjoyable as their favorite tunes.

In the rhythm of the ever-evolving cryptocurrency market, staying informed without being tethered to your trading desk is akin to catching the highlights of a music festival from the comfort of your home. Alerts and notifications serve as your personal backstage pass, giving you real-time insights into price movements, news releases, and significant market events without the need for constant monitoring. This system not only streamlines the flow of information but also ensures you're always in the loop, ready to make informed decisions. Let's delve into the benefits of these digital lookouts in the world of crypto trading.

Stay Ahead of the Market

Setting up alerts for price movements is like having a spotter in the lookout tower, alerting you to approaching opportunities or potential threats. Whether it's a sudden spike in the price of Bitcoin or a dramatic drop in an altcoin you've been eyeing, these alerts ensure you can react swiftly, capitalizing on opportunities to buy low or sell high. This proactive stance helps you stay a beat ahead in the market's fast-paced dance.

Make Informed Decisions

Beyond price alerts, notifications about news releases and significant market events are crucial for contextual trading decisions. In a market where sentiment can shift with the latest headline, being promptly informed about regulatory changes, technological advancements, or shifts in investor sentiment can significantly impact your strategy. These alerts act like the chorus in a song, guiding the melody of your trading decisions in harmony with the market's evolving narrative.

Customize Your Information Flow

One of the key benefits of alerts and notifications is the ability to customize the flow of information to match your trading interests and strategies. Much like creating a personalized playlist, you can set alerts for specific cryptocurrencies, price thresholds, and news categories. This customization ensures that you're not overwhelmed by the noise of irrelevant data, focusing instead on the tunes that matter most to you.

Save Time and Reduce Stress

Constantly monitoring the market can be both time-consuming and stressful, akin to trying to catch every performance at a festival. Alerts and notifications alleviate this pressure by bringing the information to you, allowing you to enjoy other activities or focus on analysis and strategy. This system supports a more balanced approach to trading, where staying informed doesn't have to come at the cost of your peace of mind or lifestyle.

Enhance Your Learning

For those who are still honing their trading skills, alerts and notifications offer a valuable learning tool. By observing how market events correlate with price movements and investor reactions, you can gain deeper insights into market dynamics. It's like listening to a wide range of music genres to develop a more refined taste; over time, you'll learn to discern the subtleties that distinguish a fleeting hype from a lasting trend.

In conclusion, leveraging alerts and notifications is akin to tuning into a finely curated broadcast of the cryptocurrency market's most crucial movements and events. This approach not only keeps you well-informed and ready to act but also enhances your trading experience by cutting down on the noise, reducing stress, and allowing you the freedom to engage with the market on your terms. Just as a well-timed notification can lead you to discover your new favorite song, it can also open the door to lucrative trading opportunities, all without the need for constant screen time.

In the symphony of cryptocurrency trading, where each asset plays its unique tune, keeping harmony among them requires a conductor's keen oversight. Portfolio trackers are the maestro's baton, enabling traders to orchestrate their investments with precision and grace. Just as a music conductor needs to see all the musicians and their cues at a glance, traders benefit immensely from having a consolidated view of their investments' performance. Let's delve into the importance of using portfolio trackers and how they simplify staying updated, reducing the hassle and allowing more time for the finer things in life.

A Unified View

Imagine trying to appreciate a symphony by listening to each instrument play in a different room. Similarly, trying to manage a diverse portfolio without a consolidated view can be overwhelming. Portfolio trackers bring all your investments into a single dashboard, providing a holistic view of your assets across various platforms and wallets. This unified perspective is crucial for making informed decisions, ensuring that no part of your portfolio is overlooked in the broader performance.

Real-Time Insights

In the fast-paced world of cryptocurrency, prices and market dynamics change with the beat of a drum. Portfolio trackers offer real-time updates on your investments, much like a live feed from a concert, ensuring you never miss a beat. Whether it's a sudden surge in an altcoin or a market-wide dip, having immediate access to this information allows you to react swiftly, adjusting your strategy to the market's rhythm.

Performance Analysis

Understanding how each asset contributes to your portfolio's overall performance is akin to recognizing each musician's role in a symphony. Portfolio trackers provide analytical tools that break down your investments by asset class, profitability, and other key metrics. This analysis helps identify which investments are the stars of your financial symphony and which may be out of tune, allowing you to make adjustments that align with your investment goals and risk tolerance.

Strategic Rebalancing

Just as a musical piece sometimes requires a change in tempo or volume to reach its crescendo, your investment portfolio may need rebalancing to meet your strategic goals. Portfolio trackers alert you when certain assets overperform or underperform, suggesting a rebalance might be in order. This feature ensures that your portfolio composition remains aligned with your desired risk exposure and investment objectives, harmonizing your strategy with the market's movements.

Time Efficiency and Stress Reduction

Monitoring multiple investments across various platforms can be as chaotic as trying to follow several musical scores at once. Portfolio trackers streamline this process, saving you time and reducing the stress associated with manual monitoring. This efficiency frees up your time for research, strategy development, or simply enjoying life's other melodies, confident that your investment performance is just a glance away.

Enhanced Decision Making

With comprehensive insights at your fingertips, portfolio trackers empower you with the confidence to make strategic decisions. They illuminate the path forward, much like a spotlight on a dark stage, highlighting opportunities for growth, areas for improvement, and moments to act. This empowered decision-making is the cornerstone of successful trading, turning the cacophony of the market into a harmonious performance.

In conclusion, the importance of using portfolio trackers in the world of cryptocurrency trading cannot be overstated. They are the maestro's baton that brings order to chaos, allowing traders to conduct their investments with the finesse and oversight of a symphony orchestra conductor. By providing a unified view, real-time insights, performance analysis, and strategic rebalancing capabilities, portfolio trackers ensure that you remain in tune with your investments' performance, all without the hassle of manual oversight.

Imagine you're lounging on a sunny beach, the waves gently lapping at the shore, your favorite tunes playing in the background, completely at ease knowing your trading is being taken care of. This is not a daydream but the reality made possible with automated trading bots in the cryptocurrency world. Like having a personal DJ who knows exactly what music to play and when, automated trading bots execute trades on your behalf based on predetermined criteria, ensuring you maintain a trading presence even when you're soaking up the sun or lost in the music. Let's delve into the mechanics, benefits, and considerations of automated trading bots, your unseen allies in the crypto markets.

The Mechanics of Automated Trading Bots

Automated trading bots are software programs designed to engage with financial exchanges directly, placing buy or sell orders on your behalf based on a predefined set of market analysis and criteria. These bots can interpret market data, calculate potential risks, and execute trades faster than a human ever could. It's akin to a set-it-and-forget-it playlist, where each song transitions smoothly based on your preferences, tempo, and the mood you've set, without needing your constant oversight.

Why Use Automated Trading Bots?

Efficiency: Bots can monitor and analyze the market conditions in multiple cryptocurrencies simultaneously, 24/7, something exceedingly difficult for human traders to accomplish, especially those wanting to enjoy life beyond the screen.

Speed: In the volatile crypto market, opportunities can come and go in the blink of an eye. Automated bots can execute trades at a speed unmatchable by manual trading, ensuring you never miss a beat.

Emotionless Trading: Bots operate based on predefined rules and logic, removing emotional decision-making from the equation. This can be particularly beneficial in avoiding common pitfalls like panic selling or greedy overbuying, ensuring your trading strategy remains consistent and disciplined.

Setting Up Your Bot: The Playlist of Trading

Setting up an automated trading bot requires a bit of upfront work, much like curating the perfect playlist for an event. You'll need to:

Choose Your Bot: There's a variety of bots available, from open-source platforms to subscription-based services. Select one that aligns with your trading strategy and technical comfort level.

Define Your Strategy: Just as you'd select songs to suit the mood of your gathering, you'll need to program your bot with instructions on when to buy, sell, or hold, based on technical indicators, market trends, or even news-based triggers.

Backtesting: Before letting your bot loose on live markets, test it against historical data to see how it would have performed. This is akin to doing a sound check before the party starts, ensuring everything runs smoothly when it's showtime.

Considerations and Risks

While automated trading bots offer numerous advantages, they're not without their risks:

Market Unpredictability: Bots follow predefined rules and can't interpret or react to unexpected market events or news with the same nuance a human might. It's like a playlist that can't adapt to the party's changing vibe on the fly.

Security Risks: As with any automated system, there's a risk of hacking or system failure. Ensuring your bot is from a reputable source and following best security practices is paramount.

Ongoing Monitoring: Though bots can significantly reduce the time you need to spend monitoring the markets, they're not a set-it-and-forget-it solution. Regular checks and adjustments based on market changes or performance are essential to ensure they continue to trade effectively.

In the crescendo of daily life and market fluctuations, automated trading bots offer a way to keep your trading strategy playing smoothly in the background, allowing you to enjoy the melody of life without missing out on the opportunities the crypto market presents. They embody the fusion of technology and strategy, working tirelessly behind the scenes to ensure your trading objectives are met, even when you're taking it easy.

Navigating the vast and noisy landscape of social media and forums for cryptocurrency insights can feel like trying to find the perfect song on a radio crowded with static. Just as curating a playlist with care can set the perfect mood for any occasion, selectively following reputable sources and influencers while filtering out the noise and hype can transform your feed into a valuable stream of information and insights. Let's explore some tips on how to fine-tune your information sources, ensuring you're tuned into the melody of meaningful content amidst the cacophony of the crypto sphere.

Identify Reputable Sources

Do Your Research: Start with a bit of background checking. Look into the history, credentials, and track record of the sources and influencers you consider following. It's like checking the reviews and ratings before adding a song to your playlist.

Quality Over Quantity: Follow sources known for their in-depth analysis, thoughtful commentary, and consistent reliability. It's better to have a handful of trusted sources than a flood of voices contributing to the noise.

Use Filters and Lists

Create Custom Lists: Platforms like Twitter allow you to curate lists based on interests or sectors. Creating a list for cryptocurrency news, another for blockchain technology, and yet another for market analysis can help keep your feed organized, much like creating different playlists for various moods or occasions.

Utilize Filters: Use platform-specific tools and filters to manage what appears in your feed. This might mean muting overly promotional content or setting up keywords that highlight discussions relevant to your interests.

Diversify Your Information Diet

Mix of Perspectives: Follow a range of voices from different corners of the crypto world—traders, analysts, developers, and enthusiasts. This diversity ensures you're exposed to a broad spectrum of insights, akin to a playlist that spans genres, enriching your understanding and appreciation of the market.

Global Views: Cryptocurrency is a global phenomenon. Following reputable sources from around the world can provide a more rounded perspective, highlighting trends and developments that might not be as prominent in your local discourse.

Stay Critical and Reflective

Verify Information: In the fast-paced world of crypto, rumors and misinformation can spread quickly. Always cross-check facts with multiple reputable sources before taking action, similar to verifying the authenticity of a rare vinyl before making a purchase.

Reflect on Value: Periodically review the sources you're following to ensure they still provide value. It's like revisiting your playlist to remove songs that no longer resonate with your taste or mood.

Engage and Interact

Join the Conversation: Don't hesitate to ask questions or engage in discussions. Constructive engagement can lead to deeper insights and connections within the community, much like sharing music recommendations with friends can lead to discovering new favorite tunes.

By curating your social media feed and forum interactions with the same care as you would a playlist for a cherished event, you can ensure that your foray into the world of cryptocurrency remains informative, insightful, and, above all, enjoyable. This curated approach to information gathering allows you to stay informed and ahead of the curve, all while keeping the noise at bay.

Just as a discerning music lover sifts through countless tracks to find those rare gems that resonate on a deeper level, navigating the vast ocean of information in the cryptocurrency world demands a mindset steeped in critical thinking. The ability to question, analyze, and discern valuable insights from mere speculation is not just a skill but a necessity in the digital age, where the line between informed analysis and noise can often blur. Let's explore how fostering a critical mindset can illuminate your path in the crypto space, ensuring that the information you encounter enriches your understanding and guides your decisions wisely.

Develop a Questioning Attitude

Approach every piece of information with a healthy dose of skepticism, not cynicism. Just as you might question the source of a sample in a new track, ask yourself:

Who is providing this information, and what might be their motive?

Is this analysis or opinion backed by verifiable data or evidence?

Could there be another side to this story or perspective that's not being presented?

Analyze the Source

The internet is a mixed tape of various voices, and not all are equal in credibility or intent. Scrutinizing the source of the information can provide clues about its reliability, much like knowing the difference between a mixtape curated by a renowned DJ versus one hastily thrown together.

Check the Track Record: Has the source been reliable in the past? Do they have a history of accurate predictions or insightful analysis?

Identify the Expertise: Does the source possess the necessary expertise or credentials in the subject matter they're discussing?

Look for Bias: Is the source pushing a particular agenda or trying to sell something?

Seek Out Diverse Perspectives

Just as a well-rounded playlist includes a variety of genres and artists, a well-informed trader seeks out diverse perspectives. Exposure to different viewpoints can challenge your assumptions and broaden your understanding, offering a more nuanced view of the market.

Engage with Contrarian Views: Listening to opinions that challenge your current beliefs can be enlightening, revealing blind spots or considerations you hadn't accounted for.

Compare Analysis: When researching a particular topic or asset, look at analyses from multiple sources to see where there's consensus or divergence.

Reflect and Digest

In the streaming age, it's easy to skip from track to track without truly listening. Similarly, in the age of information overload, it's vital to take a moment to reflect on the information consumed.

Take Notes: Jotting down key points can help consolidate your understanding and facilitate deeper reflection.

Discuss with Peers: Conversations with fellow traders or enthusiasts can provide additional insights and help further refine your understanding.

Stay Informed, Not Influenced

Ultimately, the goal of critical thinking is to stay informed without being unduly influenced by the prevailing winds of opinion. It's about building a conviction in your analysis and decisions, supported by evidence and reasoned judgment, much like how a connoisseur appreciates the nuances of a rare vintage or a complex symphony.

By cultivating a mindset that questions, analyzes, and seeks to understand, you arm yourself against the speculative noise that pervades much of the online discourse in cryptocurrency. This critical approach not only aids in distinguishing valuable insights from mere speculation but also fosters a deeper, more meaningful engagement with the dynamic and evolving landscape of crypto trading.

Engaging with online communities in the cryptocurrency space is akin to jamming with a band. Each member brings their unique style and insights, contributing to a richer, more harmonious collective experience. Whether it's a forum, social media platform, or messaging app, these communities can be goldmines of information, support, and inspiration. However, like any ensemble, the key to a successful collaboration lies in how you engage and contribute. Let's explore strategies for engaging with online communities in a way that enriches your trading knowledge, shares your experiences, and fosters a supportive network.

Listen Before You Speak

Just as you would listen to the other musicians in a jam session before jumping in, take the time to understand the community's vibe, rules, and the types of discussions that take place. This initial observation period helps you get a feel for how the community operates and what you can contribute.

Share Your Insights and Learnings

Once you're comfortable, start sharing your own insights and experiences. Whether it's a successful trade, a hard-learned lesson, or a piece of analysis you're proud of, your contributions add value to the collective knowledge pool. Think of it as adding your own riff to a song, enhancing the overall piece.

Ask Questions and Seek Advice

Every musician, no matter how skilled, can learn something new. Don't be afraid to ask questions or seek advice from more experienced community members. Framing your questions thoughtfully and showing that you've done some initial research will likely lead to more detailed and helpful responses.

Offer Support and Encouragement

Just as applause and encouragement can boost a performer's confidence, offering support and positive feedback to others can foster a nurturing environment. Congratulate others on their successes, offer consolation for their setbacks, and provide constructive feedback when asked. This supportive atmosphere encourages sharing and growth within the community.

Engage in Constructive Debate

Music, much like trading, is subjective, and differing opinions are inevitable. Engaging in constructive debate can be incredibly enriching, exposing you to new perspectives and strategies. Approach disagreements with respect and openness, focusing on the exchange of ideas rather than winning an argument.

Stay Humble and Open-Minded

No matter how much success you achieve, there's always more to learn. Staying humble and open-minded allows you to absorb new information and adapt to the ever-changing market. It's the willingness to continually refine your craft that separates the great musicians from the good ones.

Protect Your Boundaries

Engaging with online communities should be enriching, not draining. Be mindful of your time and emotional investment, and don't hesitate to step back or disengage if interactions become negative or overwhelming. It's important to maintain a healthy balance between online engagement and other aspects of your life.

By engaging with online communities in these ways, you not only enrich your own trading journey but also contribute to the growth and positivity of the broader cryptocurrency ecosystem. It's through sharing experiences, knowledge, and support that the community becomes stronger, more resilient, and more harmonious, much like a band that thrives on the collective talents and energies of its members.

In the digital age, where the volume of information is akin to a relentless wave crashing over us, managing information overload becomes crucial, especially in the dynamic world of cryptocurrency trading. It's like trying to find a melody in a cacophony of sounds; without a way to filter and focus, it's easy to get lost. Just as a DJ sifts through tracks to find those that truly resonate, traders must develop strategies to navigate the sea of information, focusing on quality over quantity to make informed decisions without becoming overwhelmed. Here are some strategies to help manage this deluge, ensuring you stay informed, focused, and above the flood of data.

Curate Your Sources

Start by curating your information sources carefully. Choose a few reputable news outlets, analysts, and platforms that align with your interests and trading strategy. It's about creating a finely tuned playlist of sources that consistently deliver value, rather than trying to listen to every song ever made.

Use Aggregators and Filters

Leverage news aggregators and social media filters to streamline the flow of information. Tools like Feedly or CryptoPanic can help consolidate news from multiple sources into a single, manageable feed, filtering out the noise and highlighting the news that matters most to you, much like using a music app to curate playlists based on your preferences.

Set Specific Times for Consumption

Designate specific times of the day for information consumption and stick to them. This could be a brief morning review to catch up on overnight developments and another in the evening to summarize the day's events. This structured approach helps prevent the constant checking that can lead to information fatigue, akin to setting aside time to enjoy music without letting it run incessantly in the background.

Practice Mindful Consumption

Approach information consumption mindfully. Ask yourself whether the content is adding value or merely adding to the noise. Being mindful about what you consume can help you stay focused on information that informs and enriches your trading decisions, similar to choosing music that enhances your mood and productivity rather than distracting you.

Take Regular Breaks

Remember to disconnect and take regular breaks. Continuous exposure to information, especially in a volatile market like cryptocurrency, can be mentally exhausting and counterproductive. Regular breaks can help reset your mind, much like a palate cleanser between courses or a rest between sets at a concert, allowing you to return refreshed and with renewed focus.

Summarize and Reflect

End your day by summarizing the key information you've consumed and reflecting on how it impacts your trading strategy. This practice can help consolidate your learning and clarify your thoughts, ensuring that the information you consume is translated into actionable insights, akin to reviewing the setlist after a concert to reflect on the experience.

Engage with a Community

Engaging with a community can also help manage information overload. Communities often highlight the most important news and trends, saving you from having to sift through everything yourself. Plus, discussions can offer new insights or perspectives on information you might have missed or misunderstood, much like sharing music discoveries with friends can introduce you to new genres or artists.

By adopting these strategies, you can navigate the vast ocean of information in the cryptocurrency market without drowning in it. Focusing on quality over quantity, structuring your information consumption, and taking time to reflect and disconnect are key to managing information overload, ensuring that the information serves you, rather than overwhelms you.

Chapter 6

Execution of Trades

When to Hit or Pass

Identifying the right entry point for a trade in the cryptocurrency market is akin to a surfer timing their paddle to catch the perfect wave. It requires an understanding of the market's rhythm, an eye for emerging patterns, and the patience to wait for that moment when everything aligns. Just as a surfer uses the ocean's signs to predict the coming of a great wave, traders can use a combination of technical indicators, analysis of trends, and an understanding of market cycles to pinpoint optimal entry points. Let's dive into how these elements come together to guide your entry strategy.

Understanding Market Cycles

Every market moves in cycles, including the cryptocurrency market. These cycles can range from major bull runs to bearish downturns and everything in between. Recognizing the phase of the market cycle you're in is crucial, as it sets the stage for identifying entry points. It's like knowing whether the tide is coming in or going out before you choose your spot on the beach.

Accumulation Phase: This is when prices are at a low following a downturn, and savvy investors start to buy, anticipating the next rise. Entering trades in this phase can be like paddling into position as you see a swell starting to build.

Expansion Phase: Here, prices start to rise, and the trend becomes more apparent. While it might feel safer to enter during this phase, the earlier you catch it, the better—much like catching a wave as it starts to form, not once it's already breaking.

Utilizing Technical Indicators

Technical indicators are the tools that help you read the market's signs and signals. They can indicate when a potential entry point is approaching, based on historical data and statistical analysis.

Moving Averages: These indicators smooth out price data over a specific period and can indicate a trend's direction. A moving average crossover, for example, where a short-term average crosses over a long-term average, can signal an opportune time to enter a trade.

Relative Strength Index (RSI): The RSI measures the magnitude of recent price changes to evaluate overbought or oversold conditions. An RSI reading below 30 suggests an asset is oversold (potentially undervalued), indicating a good entry point.

Volume: High trading volume can confirm the strength of a price move. An uptick in volume alongside a price increase can suggest the move has support and might be a good time to enter.

Analyzing Trends

Trend analysis involves identifying the direction the market is moving. Is it in an uptrend, downtrend, or moving sideways? Trends can be your roadmap to finding entry points.

Uptrend: Characterized by higher highs and higher lows. Look for pullbacks or retracements as potential entry points, where the price dips before continuing its upward trajectory.

Downtrend: Marked by lower lows and lower highs. Opportunities might arise during a corrective bounce, where the price temporarily reverses before continuing down.

Sideways Trend: Here, the market is in consolidation. Entry points might be found at the upper and lower bounds of the price range, buying at support levels and selling at resistance levels.

In conclusion, identifying the optimal entry points for trades requires a blend of understanding market cycles, utilizing technical indicators, and analyzing trends. Just like catching the perfect wave, it's about timing, insight, and sometimes, a bit of patience and bravery. By combining these elements, you can position yourself to enter trades at moments that offer a favorable balance of risk and potential reward, riding the market's momentum to your advantage.

Just as knowing when to gracefully exit the dance floor before the song ends can preserve the perfect night out, setting strategic exit points for your trades ensures you lock in profits or cut losses before the market shifts against you. In the unpredictable rhythm of cryptocurrency trading, having clear exit strategies is crucial. These strategies enable you to manage your trades dynamically, responding to market changes with finesse rather than panic. Let's explore various techniques for setting exit points, including stop-loss orders and trailing stops, that can help you dance in tune with the market's beat.

Setting Profit Targets

Profit targets are predetermined levels at which you close your position to capture gains. Establishing these targets requires an understanding of market structure, resistance levels, and your risk-reward ratio. It's akin to knowing your evening's peak moment, ensuring you leave on a high note.

Resistance Levels: These are points where the price has historically struggled to break through. Setting your profit target just before these levels can maximize your chances of exiting before a potential pullback.

Risk-Reward Ratio: This ratio helps determine your profit target based on the risk you're taking. For instance, with a 1:3 risk-reward ratio, if you're risking $100 on a trade, you'd set your profit target to make $300.

Using Stop-Loss Orders

Stop-loss orders are essential tools for managing risk, automatically closing out your position at a predetermined price to prevent further losses. They act as a safety net, ensuring that a bad trade doesn't turn into a catastrophic loss, much like deciding in advance how late you'll stay out before it's too late.

Fixed Stop-Loss: Set at a specific price level when you enter the trade. It's determined based on technical analysis, such as below a support level or a certain percentage from the entry price.

Mental Stop-Loss: While not an actual order, a mental stop-loss is a price level you commit to exiting a trade, requiring discipline to execute without hesitation.

Implementing Trailing Stops

Trailing stops are dynamic exit strategies that allow profits to run while still providing downside protection. As the trade moves in your favor, the trailing stop adjusts itself, maintaining a predetermined distance from the market price. It's like auto-adjusting your speed on the dance floor to match the music's tempo, ensuring you're always in sync.

Percentage-Based: The trailing stop is set at a certain percentage away from the current market price. If the price moves favorably, the trailing stop moves with it, locking in profits if the market reverses.

Volatility-Based: Utilizes market volatility to set the trailing distance, often employing indicators like the Average True Range (ATR) to gauge market conditions and adjust the stop accordingly.

The Art of Letting Go

A critical aspect of exit strategies is knowing when to let go. Holding onto a position out of attachment or hope, despite all signs pointing to an exit, can erode profits or deepen losses. It's like staying on the dance floor long after the music has stopped being enjoyable, missing the cue that it's time to rest.

In conclusion, setting exit points is about balancing optimism for a trade's potential with the pragmatism of securing profits and minimizing losses. Whether through profit targets, stop-loss orders, or trailing stops, these strategies offer a structured approach to navigating the ebb and flow of the markets. By planning your exits as carefully as your entries, you can trade with confidence, knowing you're prepared to step gracefully to the sidelines, regardless of how the market turns.

Patience in trading is an art form akin to the anticipation and satisfaction of waiting for the chorus to drop in your favorite song. In both realms, the buildup is essential, and the payoff is often worth the wait. In the fast-paced world of cryptocurrency trading, where the market's tempo can shift from adagio to allegro in a matter of moments, the virtue of patience is not just valuable; it's vital. Let's explore the nuanced role of patience in trading and how it parallels the patience required in appreciating a beautifully composed piece of music.

The Buildup to the Chorus: Recognizing Market Setups

Just as a song builds up to its chorus, market conditions often set the stage before a significant move. This buildup can manifest in various technical patterns, sentiment indicators, or macroeconomic factors aligning, signaling an impending shift. The key lies in recognizing these setups and understanding that, much like the anticipation of a musical crescendo, not every moment is right for action. The ability to wait for these conditions to align before executing a trade mirrors the patience of listening to a song's verses and bridges, knowing that the chorus will bring the emotional and climactic payoff.

The Drop: Capitalizing on the Moment

When the chorus drops, the wait pays off with a rush of energy and emotion. In trading, this moment comes when all indicators align, signaling a strong entry or exit point. Acting in haste or impatience can lead to missed opportunities or entering trades based on incomplete setups, much like the disappointment of a song peaking prematurely or the chorus not delivering on the buildup's promise. Patience ensures that when you do make a move, it's both calculated and timely, capitalizing on the market's rhythm at its peak moment.

The Quiet After the Chorus: Reflection and Anticipation

After the chorus comes a period of reflection and anticipation of what's next. In trading, after executing a trade, there's a similar phase of monitoring and reflection, considering the next move as the market continues to unfold. Just as enjoying a song involves appreciating its entirety—not just the chorus—successful trading involves a continuous cycle of analysis, action, and anticipation, always with an eye towards the next opportunity.

Cultivating Patience

Cultivating patience in trading involves several practices:

Setting Realistic Expectations: Understand that not every day or session will offer ideal trading opportunities. Much like not every song becomes a hit, not every market movement is worth the trade.

Developing a Comprehensive Strategy: A well-thought-out trading strategy that includes criteria for entry, exit, and risk management can help you stay focused and patient, much like a well-composed song that engages the listener from start to finish.

Practicing Mindfulness: Just as listening to music can be a meditative experience, bringing mindfulness into your trading practice can help you remain patient and centered, focusing on the present and waiting for the right moment to act.

Conclusion

Patience in trading, as in music, enriches the experience and often leads to the most rewarding outcomes. By understanding the rhythm of the market, waiting for the right setup, and acting decisively when the moment arrives, you can trade in harmony with the market's dynamics. Just as the anticipation of the chorus enhances the joy of the drop, patience in trading magnifies the satisfaction and success of well-timed actions.

In the whirlwind world of cryptocurrency trading, where the markets pulse with an unceasing rhythm, mindfulness and meditation emerge as sanctuaries of calm, helping traders to anchor their thoughts and emotions amidst the storm. Just as a musician might center themselves before a performance, traders can use mindfulness exercises and meditation techniques to foster a state of calm clarity, enhancing decision-making processes and emotional resilience. Here are some tailored practices designed to help traders navigate the markets with a composed mind and a steady heart.

Breathing Exercises

Focused Breathing: Begin by finding a comfortable, quiet space. Close your eyes and take a deep breath in through your nose, filling your lungs completely, then slowly exhale through your mouth. Concentrate on the sensation of the air moving in and out of your body. This simple act of focused breathing can help clear the mind of noise and center your thoughts, much like tuning an instrument before playing.

Counting Breaths: Inhale deeply while silently counting to four, hold your breath for a count of four, then exhale smoothly over another count of four. This technique, known as the "4-4-4" breathing exercise, can help reduce stress and improve focus, preparing you for the decisions ahead.

Visualization Techniques

The Calm Ocean Visualization: Imagine yourself sitting on a serene beach at sunset, watching the gentle waves roll in and out. With each wave's ebb, envision any stress or tension leaving your body, and with each flow, imagine calmness washing over you. This visualization can help cultivate a sense of peace and stability, essential for navigating the volatile crypto markets.

The Mountain Stance Visualization: Picture yourself as a mountain, tall and steadfast. Visualize the markets' volatility as the changing weather around the mountain—storms may rage, and winds may howl, but the mountain remains unshaken. This exercise fosters a sense of inner strength and resilience, empowering you to remain composed under pressure.

Mindful Awareness Practices

Mindful Observation: Choose an object within your sight and focus all your attention on it. Observe it without judgment, noting its colors, shapes, and texture. This practice of mindful observation can sharpen your focus and bring your mind back to the present moment, away from the anxiety of potential future market movements.

The Five Senses Exercise: Take a moment to notice five things you can see, four things you can touch, three things you can hear, two things you can smell, and one thing you can taste. This exercise grounds you in the present moment, helping to dispel stress and enhance decision-making clarity.

Regular Meditation Practice

Daily Meditation: Dedicate a specific time each day to meditate, starting with just a few minutes and gradually increasing the duration. Use guided meditations designed for focus and stress reduction, available through apps or online platforms, to ease into the practice.

Walking Meditation: If sitting still is challenging, try walking meditation. Walk slowly and deliberately, fully aware of each step and the sensations in your body. This can be particularly useful for breaking up long periods of screen time, refreshing both mind and body.

Incorporating these mindfulness exercises and meditation techniques into your daily routine can significantly enhance your trading practice. By fostering a state of mental clarity and emotional equilibrium, you're not just better prepared to face the markets' ebbs and flows; you're also investing in your overall well-being, ensuring that your trading journey is both prosperous and fulfilling.

Creating a supportive trading environment is akin to setting the stage for a performance, where every element is meticulously arranged to promote harmony, focus, and well-being. In the realm of cryptocurrency trading, where the tempo can shift rapidly, ensuring your trading space is a haven of calm can significantly influence your mental agility and emotional resilience. Let's explore how incorporating elements such as music, aromatherapy, and ergonomic design can transform your trading area into a sanctuary that nurtures calmness and reduces stress.

Harmonize with Music

Music has the profound ability to influence mood and cognitive performance. Curating a playlist that resonates with your trading tempo can help maintain focus, elevate mood, or instill calm.

Focus-enhancing tunes: Instrumental music or ambient sounds can help minimize distractions and enhance concentration. Consider classical music or lo-fi beats, known for their soothing yet focus-inducing properties.

Mood-lifting melodies: On days when the market is gloomy, uplifting music can be the nudge needed to maintain a positive outlook. Choose tracks that bring you joy and energy, akin to a musical pep talk.

Aromatherapy for the Senses

The olfactory system has a direct pathway to the brain's limbic system, which governs emotions and memory. Utilizing aromatherapy can subtly shift the atmosphere of your trading space, promoting relaxation or alertness.

Lavender for calm: Known for its stress-reducing qualities, diffusing lavender oil can help create a tranquil trading environment.

Peppermint to invigorate: For moments when you need a mental boost, the invigorating scent of peppermint can enhance alertness and concentration.

Ergonomic Considerations

The physical comfort of your trading environment is paramount. Ergonomic considerations can prevent physical strain and fatigue, ensuring your body isn't a distraction.

Supportive seating: Invest in a quality chair that supports proper posture. Look for adjustable features to tailor the fit to your body, reducing the risk of back pain or discomfort.

Monitor height and distance: Position your monitor(s) at eye level and at an appropriate distance to avoid straining your neck or eyes. The top of the screen should be at or slightly below eye level.

Keyboard and mouse placement: Ensure your keyboard and mouse are placed in a way that allows your wrists to remain straight and your arms at or below elbow level, minimizing the risk of strain.

Personalizing Your Space

Natural light and plants: Incorporate elements of nature into your trading space. Natural light boosts mood and alertness, while plants can improve air quality and provide a visual rest from screen time.

Personal touches: Adding personal items that bring you joy or inspiration can make your space feel comforting and motivating. Whether it's a photo of a cherished memory, a motivational quote, or a piece of art, these touches can make your trading environment uniquely yours.

Routine and Rituals

Start-of-day rituals: Begin your trading day with a ritual that sets a positive tone. This might include meditation, stretching, or reviewing your trading plan. Rituals can signal to your brain that it's time to focus.

End-of-day decompression: Establish a routine to wind down from trading, helping to separate your work from personal time. This could be a brief walk, reading, or any activity that helps you relax and decompress.

Creating a trading environment that promotes calmness and reduces stress is about more than just aesthetics; it's about crafting a space that supports your mental and physical well-being, enhancing your ability to trade with clarity and purpose. By integrating music, aromatherapy, ergonomic design, and personal touches, your trading space can become a sanctuary of calm in the dynamic world of cryptocurrency trading, ensuring that you're not only performing at your best but also enjoying the journey.

Emotional management in trading is akin to maintaining composure during an intense performance. The cryptocurrency market, with its crescendos of highs and decrescendos of lows, can stir a symphony of emotions, from exhilaration to despair. Recognizing and managing these emotional responses is crucial for maintaining objectivity and focus. Here are strategies to help you conduct your trading decisions with clarity, ensuring your emotions enhance rather than impede your performance.

Recognize Your Emotional Cues

Self-Awareness: Begin by tuning into your emotional responses during different market conditions. Note feelings of anxiety, excitement, or frustration as they arise, akin to identifying the specific instruments in a piece of music that evoke certain emotions.

Journaling: Keep a trading journal that includes not only your trades and strategies but also your emotional state during those trades. Over time, this can help you identify patterns in your emotional responses and the market conditions that trigger them.

Establish a Pre-Trade Routine

Mindfulness Practices: Engage in mindfulness or meditation before trading to center yourself. This can be as simple as a few minutes of deep breathing exercises to calm the mind and reduce stress, similar to an artist taking a moment of silence before stepping onto the stage.

Review Your Trading Plan: Remind yourself of your trading plan and the rules you've set for entry, exit, and risk management. This acts as a rehearsal, grounding your actions in strategy rather than emotion.

Set Emotional Boundaries

Define Acceptable Losses: Before entering a trade, decide on an acceptable level of loss you're comfortable with. This predetermined boundary can help prevent emotional decision-making in response to market movements.

Take Breaks: Regularly step away from the markets to clear your head, especially after a stressful trading session. This is akin to taking an intermission during a concert to refresh and refocus.

Embrace a Growth Mindset

Learn from Losses: View losses as learning opportunities rather than failures. Analyzing what went wrong and how you can improve for next time shifts the perspective from emotional to analytical, fostering growth.

Celebrate Wins Wisely: While it's important to acknowledge successes, avoid overexuberance. Reflect on what strategies worked and why, ensuring that each win contributes to your trading wisdom.

Cultivate Support Networks

Engage with Community: Connect with other traders to share experiences and strategies. A supportive community can provide perspective, reduce feelings of isolation, and offer constructive feedback.

Professional Support: Consider seeking the guidance of a trading coach or a therapist, especially if emotions are significantly impacting your trading decisions or quality of life.

Practice Gratitude and Perspective

Gratitude Journaling: Regularly note things you're grateful for, both in trading and other aspects of life. This can shift focus from what's lacking to what's abundant, fostering a positive outlook.

Long-Term Perspective: Remind yourself of your long-term goals and vision. Market movements are just one part of a broader journey. Maintaining this perspective can help smooth the emotional highs and lows.

Managing emotions in trading isn't about suppression but about recognition, regulation, and channeling these feelings in ways that support your trading goals. By implementing these strategies, you can ensure that your emotional responses become assets rather than obstacles, allowing you to navigate the markets with the poise of a seasoned performer, attuned to the rhythm of your trading strategy and the dynamics of the cryptocurrency market.

Analyzing trading mistakes and losses is akin to reviewing a recording of a performance to understand where the missteps occurred and how to improve for the next show. In the volatile world of cryptocurrency trading, losses are inevitable, but they need not be futile. Instead, they can serve as invaluable learning experiences, guiding your growth and refinement as a trader. Here's how to constructively review and analyze your trading mistakes, turning setbacks into stepping stones for future success.

Embrace a Learning Mindset

Begin with the perspective that every loss is a lesson in disguise. This mindset shifts the focus from dwelling on the negative to identifying opportunities for growth, much like a musician listens for off-key notes to improve future performances.

Detailed Journaling

Maintain a detailed trading journal that goes beyond the numbers. For each trade, record your strategy, market conditions, your emotional state, and the rationale behind your decisions. When a trade doesn't go as planned, this journal becomes a treasure trove of insights, revealing not just what went wrong, but why.

Objective Analysis

Approach the analysis of your mistakes with the detachment of a scientist studying an experiment. Ask yourself:

What was my initial strategy, and did I adhere to it?

Were my entry and exit points based on solid analysis or emotion?

Did I properly assess the risk and set appropriate stop-losses?

How did external factors or news influence my decisions?

Seek Patterns

Over time, review your journal to identify patterns in your trading behavior that lead to losses. Common patterns might include overtrading in response to losses, failing to adjust stop-loss orders, or repeatedly falling for the same market traps. Recognizing these patterns is the first step in breaking them.

Feedback Loops

Don't hesitate to seek feedback from more experienced traders or mentors. Sharing your analysis and getting an external perspective can uncover blind spots and offer new strategies or approaches you might not have considered.

Educate and Adapt

Use your findings to educate yourself further. If you find that a particular aspect of market analysis is repeatedly tripping you up, dive deeper into studying that area. Adapt your trading plan based on the lessons learned, whether it means refining your entry and exit criteria, adjusting your risk management strategies, or developing new rules to govern your trading behavior.

Practice Forgiveness

Be kind to yourself. Trading is a skill honed over time, and even the most seasoned traders make mistakes. Forgiving yourself for missteps is crucial for maintaining the confidence and resilience needed to continue trading.

Implement Changes Gradually

Integrate the lessons learned into your trading strategy incrementally. Massive overhauls can be overwhelming and difficult to evaluate. Small, manageable changes allow for easier tracking of their impact on your trading performance.

Revisit Successful Trades

Balance your review by also analyzing trades that went well. Understanding why a trade was successful can reinforce positive trading habits and strategies, serving as a reminder of what you're capable of achieving when you apply your insights and knowledge.

Constructively analyzing trading mistakes transforms them from mere setbacks into powerful catalysts for growth and improvement. This process ensures that each loss contributes to your development as a trader, building a foundation of experience that will inform and guide your future trading decisions. Just as musicians learn and evolve with every performance, so too can traders refine their craft with each trade, turning every mistake into a stepping stone towards mastery.

Maintaining perspective on losses is crucial in the tumultuous world of cryptocurrency trading, where the swings can be dramatic and the lessons hard-earned. Viewing losses through a constructive lens can transform them from setbacks into vital tuition in the university of market wisdom. Just as an artist invests in materials and time, sometimes with works that never see the light of day, traders must view losses as an investment in their education and growth. Here are techniques to help keep losses in perspective, enabling you to embrace them as part of the learning process rather than as failures.

Recognize Losses as Part of the Process

Acceptance: Understand that losses are an inevitable part of trading. No strategy guarantees 100% success, much like no artist creates a masterpiece with every stroke. Accepting this reality helps temper expectations and reduces the sting of individual losses.

The Tuition Concept

Investment in Learning: Reframe losses as tuition for the invaluable lessons the market teaches. Each loss is a payment toward your education in market dynamics, risk management, and emotional control. This perspective encourages a growth mindset, where the focus is on learning and improvement.

Historical Context

Study Market History: Familiarize yourself with the history of the markets and the stories of successful traders. Many have faced significant losses and periods of doubt before achieving success. Understanding that your experiences are part of a larger narrative can provide comfort and motivation.

Relative Scale

Keep Losses in Perspective: Compare your losses to the overall size of your trading account, and remember your long-term goals. A loss that seems significant today may be a small blip in the context of your entire trading journey.

Balanced Portfolio

Diversification: Ensure your investment strategy includes diversification. A balanced portfolio can help mitigate the impact of losses in any single trade or asset class, much like a varied repertoire allows a musician to appeal to a broader audience.

Focus on the Process, Not Just Outcomes

Process Over Outcomes: Concentrate on refining your trading process and decision-making criteria. Consistently applying a well-thought-out strategy is more important for long-term success than the outcome of any single trade.

Mindfulness and Emotional Balance

Mindfulness Practices: Engage in mindfulness and stress-reduction techniques. Practices like meditation, exercise, or engaging in hobbies can help restore emotional balance and clear thinking, enabling you to view losses with equanimity.

Create a Support System

Seek Support: Build a network of fellow traders and mentors. Sharing experiences, especially losses, can offer new insights, reinforce the normalcy of setbacks, and provide emotional support.

Celebrate Wins and Learning Equally

Acknowledge Growth: Take time to celebrate the wins, but also the learning that comes from losses. Acknowledging growth in knowledge and skill is crucial for maintaining morale and motivation.

Reflect and Reset

Regular Reviews: Periodically review your trades, both successful and not, to assess what worked and what didn't. This reflection is an opportunity to reset goals and strategies based on what you've learned.

By keeping losses in perspective and viewing them as part of your education and growth as a trader, you can navigate the emotional ups and downs of the market with greater resilience. This approach not only aids in emotional management but also in honing your skills and strategies for future success. Remember, in the grand composition of your trading career, each loss is a note that contributes to the broader melody of your journey.

Building emotional resilience in trading is akin to maintaining your groove even after the music stops; it's about finding your rhythm again, confident that the next tune will play. The cryptocurrency market, with its inherent volatility, can test even the most stoic trader, making resilience not just beneficial but essential for long-term success. Developing this resilience involves cultivating a mindset and practices that enable you to face setbacks with grit and grace, ensuring that each challenge strengthens rather than diminishes your resolve. Here's advice on fortifying your emotional resilience and keeping a positive outlook through the market's inevitable ups and downs.

Embrace the Cycle of Market Emotions

Understand that the market moves in cycles, not just in terms of price, but also in the emotions it elicits. Accepting this as a natural part of trading helps prepare you for the rollercoaster, reducing the shock when downturns occur and keeping euphoria in check during highs.

Cultivate a Growth Mindset

Focus on Learning: View every market interaction as an opportunity to learn. Whether it's a win, a loss, or a draw, there's always a lesson to be gleaned. This focus on continuous improvement builds resilience by valuing progress over perfection.

Embrace Challenges: See challenges as puzzles to be solved rather than insurmountable obstacles. This approach fosters resilience by framing difficulties as opportunities for growth.

Maintain a Long-Term Perspective

Zoom out and consider the broader picture of your trading journey. Short-term setbacks are less daunting when viewed as small bumps on a longer road. Remembering your long-term goals and the reasons you started trading can help sustain motivation and perspective.

Practice Self-Care and Mindfulness

Regularly engage in activities that reduce stress and enhance well-being, such as exercise, meditation, or pursuing hobbies. Mindfulness practices can also help you remain present and grounded, mitigating the anxiety that future uncertainties may bring.

Keep a Positive but Realistic Outlook

Optimism is a powerful tool for resilience, but it must be tempered with realism. Hope for the best while preparing for the worst, ensuring your optimism is informed and actionable, not just wishful thinking.

Develop a Supportive Network

Surround yourself with a community of fellow traders and individuals who uplift and support you. Sharing experiences, especially during challenging times, can provide solace, alternative perspectives, and the strength to persevere.

Reflect and Reset Regularly

Take time to reflect on your trading decisions, the outcomes, and the emotional responses they elicited. This reflection is crucial for learning and adapting your strategies. Regularly resetting your goals and expectations based on these insights can reinforce resilience by aligning your efforts with current realities.

Celebrate the Wins, No Matter How Small

Acknowledging and celebrating successes, no matter how small, reinforces a positive outlook and builds resilience. These moments of recognition nourish your motivation, reminding you of your capabilities and progress.

Learn to Detach from the Outcome

While easier said than done, learning to detach your self-worth from your trading performance is vital for resilience. Your value as a person is not defined by wins or losses in the market. This separation helps maintain emotional equilibrium regardless of market conditions.

Stay Flexible and Adaptive

The only constant in the cryptocurrency market is change. Staying flexible and open to adjusting your strategies in response to new information or market dynamics is crucial for resilience. It's about dancing to the market's evolving rhythm, ready to change your steps as the music shifts.

Building emotional resilience in trading is a continuous process, requiring patience, introspection, and a commitment to growth. By embracing these practices, you can develop the fortitude to navigate the market's highs and lows, maintaining your groove and positivity through every tune the market plays.

Chapter 7

Diversifying Your Portfolio Like a Stoner's Snack Drawer

The inherent volatility of the cryptocurrency market is like the unpredictability of a weather system in fast-forward; sunny skies can turn stormy in minutes, and vice versa. This characteristic, while part of the allure for many traders, also underscores the risk of a single-asset strategy. Just as relying on one type of snack can leave you unsatisfied if your mood changes, putting all your investments into one cryptocurrency can expose you to significant risks when market conditions shift. Let's delve into how market volatility can impact a single-asset strategy and why diversification is crucial.

The Nature of Crypto Volatility

Cryptocurrency markets are renowned for their swift and dramatic price movements. Several factors contribute to this volatility:

Market Sentiment: Crypto markets are highly sensitive to news and social media trends. A single tweet or news article can trigger rapid buying or selling.

Liquidity: Compared to traditional markets, some crypto assets have lower liquidity, meaning fewer buyers and sellers. This can lead to larger price swings as transactions have a more pronounced impact on the market price.

Regulatory News: Announcements of regulatory changes or government stances on cryptocurrencies in various countries can lead to significant price fluctuations.

The Risk of a Single-Asset Strategy

Investing solely in one cryptocurrency, no matter how promising, amplifies your exposure to these volatile conditions. Consider the following risks:

Concentration Risk: Just like a diet based on a single food group can lead to health issues, a portfolio concentrated in one asset lacks nutritional balance. If the chosen asset plummets, your entire investment faces significant devaluation.

Missed Opportunities: Focusing on one asset means missing out on potential gains from other cryptocurrencies or asset classes. Diversification allows you to capture growth across a broader spectrum of opportunities.

Emotional Decision-Making: High volatility can lead to stress and emotional decision-making. When your entire investment rides on the performance of a single asset, the temptation to make hasty decisions in response to short-term market movements increases.

The Case for Diversification

Diversification is the investment equivalent of a balanced diet. Just as variety in food intake can buffer against nutritional deficiencies and provide a more enjoyable eating experience, a diversified investment portfolio can mitigate risk and enhance potential returns. Here's how diversification counters the risks of volatility:

Risk Reduction: By spreading your investment across multiple assets, you reduce the impact of any single asset's poor performance on your overall portfolio.

Exposure to Different Market Cycles: Different assets may perform well at different times, smoothing out returns over time. While one asset might be experiencing a downturn, another could be on the upswing.

Emotional Equilibrium: A diversified portfolio can provide a sense of security and reduce the temptation to react hastily to market fluctuations, promoting more rational, long-term focused decision-making.

In summary, the volatility of the cryptocurrency market, while offering the potential for high returns, underscores the risks of a single-asset strategy. Diversifying your portfolio is akin to packing a snack drawer with a variety of options; it prepares you for different cravings and reduces the risk of disappointment. By spreading your investments across a range of assets, you can navigate the market's ups and downs more smoothly, maintaining your financial health and peace of mind amidst the turbulence.

In the intricate tapestry of cryptocurrency trading, external factors such as regulatory changes or technological issues can act like sudden jolts to the system, disproportionately impacting a single investment much like an unexpected storm can ruin a planned outdoor concert. These unforeseen events, often beyond the control of individual investors, underscore the risks of concentrating one's capital in a single asset. By examining how these factors can influence the market, traders can better appreciate the protective buffer diversification offers.

Regulatory Changes

The regulatory landscape for cryptocurrencies remains a patchwork of global jurisdictions, each with its own stance and pace of regulation. When regulatory bodies in significant markets announce new policies or enforcement actions, the impact can be swift and severe, particularly on specific cryptocurrencies:

Legal Status: Changes in the legal status of cryptocurrencies, bans, or stringent regulations in key markets can lead to immediate and sharp declines in value. If your portfolio is heavily weighted towards a cryptocurrency that falls out of regulatory favor, the losses can be significant.

Compliance Costs: New compliance requirements can impose financial and operational burdens on blockchain projects, affecting their viability and, consequently, the value of associated tokens. A diversified portfolio can mitigate the risk exposure to any single project's regulatory hurdles.

Technological Issues

The fast-evolving nature of blockchain technology means that cryptocurrencies and their underlying platforms are continually being updated and tested, sometimes revealing vulnerabilities:

Security Breaches: High-profile hacks or security breaches can lead to immediate loss of investor confidence and value. If your investment is concentrated in an asset that experiences a breach, the impact can be devastating.

Network Forks: Significant updates or disagreements within a cryptocurrency's community can lead to forks, creating new versions of the currency. This can dilute the value of the original asset or lead to market uncertainty, affecting its price.

Market Manipulation

In the relatively unregulated expanse of the crypto market, manipulation by influential players can lead to drastic price fluctuations:

Pump and Dump Schemes: These schemes can inflate the price of a cryptocurrency artificially before those in control sell off, crashing the price and leaving uninformed investors with losses.

Whale Movements: Large holders of a cryptocurrency, known as whales, can significantly influence market prices with their trading decisions, disproportionately impacting smaller investors who might be overexposed to a single asset.

The Protective Shield of Diversification

Diversification acts as a protective shield, spreading the risk across various assets so that the impact of negative events on any single investment is lessened:

Geographic Diversification: By investing in cryptocurrencies that operate in different global jurisdictions, you can mitigate the risk associated with regulatory changes in any single country.

Technological Spread: Diversifying across cryptocurrencies built on different blockchain technologies or platforms can reduce the risk tied to technological vulnerabilities or forks in any single blockchain.

Sector Diversification: Expanding your portfolio beyond cryptocurrencies into other asset classes can provide a buffer against crypto-specific risks, including market manipulation.

In essence, while unforeseen events are a natural part of the financial landscape, their impact can be mitigated through strategic diversification. Just as a music festival might spread its headline acts across various stages to ensure that an issue with one doesn't ruin the entire show, a well-diversified portfolio can help ensure that external shocks don't derail your financial goals.

Venturing beyond the dominion of Bitcoin and Ethereum, the cryptocurrency universe is teeming with a diverse array of altcoins and tokens, each offering unique propositions, technologies, and opportunities. Much like a snack drawer filled with a variety of flavors and textures, the altcoin and token market caters to a wide range of tastes and investment strategies. This section will explore the colorful world of altcoins and tokens, highlighting their differences from major cryptocurrencies and the unique opportunities they present for diversifying your portfolio.

Understanding Altcoins

Altcoins, or alternative coins, encompass all cryptocurrencies other than Bitcoin. Created in the wake of Bitcoin's success, altcoins seek to improve upon or offer different use cases than Bitcoin. Here's what makes them stand out:

Innovation and Variety: Altcoins come in many forms, with some focusing on enhanced privacy features, like Monero and Zcash, others on scalability solutions, like Cardano and Solana, and yet more on specific sectors like finance (DeFi coins) or entertainment (social media tokens).

Opportunity for High Returns: Due to their lower market capitalization compared to Bitcoin, altcoins can offer higher potential returns. Early investment in promising altcoins can lead to significant gains as the projects mature and gain wider adoption.

Increased Risk: With high potential returns comes increased volatility and risk. Altcoins are more susceptible to market sentiment, regulatory news, and competition within the cryptocurrency space.

Exploring Tokens

Tokens represent a broader category of digital assets created on existing blockchain platforms. Unlike altcoins, which have their own independent blockchains, tokens operate on top of a platform's blockchain, like Ethereum, which hosts a multitude of tokens thanks to its smart contract capabilities.

Utility Tokens: These tokens provide access to a product or service offered by the project. For example, Filecoin tokens allow users to buy and sell storage space on its decentralized storage network.

Security Tokens: Representing investment in a real-world asset or enterprise, security tokens are subject to regulatory oversight, akin to traditional securities. They offer a bridge between the blockchain world and the traditional finance sector.

Governance Tokens: Offering holders the right to vote on decisions that affect the project, governance tokens are central to decentralized autonomous organizations (DAOs) and other decentralized projects.

Unique Opportunities

Diversification: Including a mix of altcoins and tokens in your portfolio can spread risk and expose you to growth in various sectors within the blockchain ecosystem.

Access to Emerging Technologies: Investing in altcoins and tokens allows you to support and be part of innovative blockchain projects and applications, from decentralized finance (DeFi) to non-fungible tokens (NFTs) and beyond.

Community and Participation: Many altcoin and token projects foster strong communities of supporters and developers, offering opportunities for engagement and direct influence on the project's direction through governance tokens.

Navigating the Altcoin and Token Landscape

While the potential for significant returns exists, navigating the altcoin and token markets requires due diligence, ongoing research, and an appetite for risk. Here are a few tips:

Research Thoroughly: Beyond market trends and price analysis, understand the project's fundamentals, including the team, technology, use case, and community support.

Stay Informed: The cryptocurrency market evolves rapidly. Regularly update your knowledge to keep pace with new developments, regulatory changes, and technological advancements.

Risk Management: Allocate only a portion of your portfolio to altcoins and tokens, balancing high-risk investments with more stable assets to manage overall risk.

Exploring the world of altcoins and tokens opens up a kaleidoscope of investment opportunities beyond the mainstream cryptocurrencies. With careful selection and a balanced approach, diversifying into these assets can add both flavor and potential for growth to your portfolio, much like the perfect mix of snacks ready to satisfy any craving.

Diversifying your investment portfolio beyond the realm of cryptocurrencies is like expanding your culinary tastes beyond your favorite snacks; it opens up a world of flavors and experiences, reducing the risk of palate fatigue and providing nutritional balance. Just as a well-rounded diet incorporates a variety of food groups, a robust investment strategy benefits from a mix of asset classes, including stocks, bonds, commodities, and real estate. Additionally, exploring emerging areas like NFTs (Non-Fungible Tokens) and DeFi (Decentralized Finance) can offer unique opportunities and exposure to the forefront of technological innovation. Let's explore these traditional and emerging asset classes to understand their role in a diversified portfolio.

Stocks

Equity Ownership: Investing in stocks means buying a share of ownership in a company. Stocks have historically provided substantial returns over the long term, though they come with market volatility and risks.

Diversification within Stocks: Even within the stock market, diversification is key. Consider a mix of sectors (technology, healthcare, energy), geographic regions (US, Europe, Emerging Markets), and company sizes (large-cap, mid-cap, small-cap).

Bonds

Fixed Income: Bonds are essentially loans you give to governments or corporations in exchange for regular interest payments, plus the return of the bond's face value at maturity. They tend to offer lower returns than stocks but come with lower risk, making them a stabilizing force in your portfolio.

Types of Bonds: Government bonds are generally considered safer than corporate bonds but offer lower interest rates. Diversifying across different types of bonds can balance risk and return.

Commodities

Tangible Assets: Commodities include physical goods like gold, silver, oil, and agricultural products. They can act as a hedge against inflation and currency devaluation, adding a layer of protection to your portfolio.

Market Factors: Commodity prices are influenced by geopolitical events, supply and demand dynamics, and currency fluctuations, presenting both opportunities and risks.

Real Estate

Tangible Property Investment: Real estate investment can range from purchasing physical properties to investing in REITs (Real Estate Investment Trusts). Real estate can provide rental income and potential appreciation in value.

Market and Location Dependence: Real estate markets can vary significantly by location, and factors such as economic conditions and interest rates can affect returns.

Emerging Areas: NFTs and DeFi

NFTs (Non-Fungible Tokens): Represent ownership or proof of authenticity of unique digital items using blockchain technology. While highly speculative, NFTs have opened up new opportunities in art, music, gaming, and collectibles.

DeFi (Decentralized Finance): DeFi uses blockchain to remove intermediaries in financial transactions, offering services like lending, borrowing, and trading through smart contracts. DeFi tokens and platforms can offer high returns but come with significant risks, including regulatory uncertainty and the potential for loss due to smart contract vulnerabilities.

Navigating Traditional and Emerging Investments

When venturing beyond cryptocurrencies, it's crucial to apply the same principles of due diligence, understanding each asset's risks and rewards, and aligning your investments with your financial goals and risk tolerance. Regularly reassessing and rebalancing your portfolio ensures it remains aligned with your investment strategy and adapts to changing market conditions.

Incorporating a mix of traditional and emerging asset classes into your investment strategy can provide not only a buffer against the volatility of the crypto market but also exposure to a broader range of economic activities and innovations. Like a well-curated snack drawer, a diversified portfolio offers a variety of tastes and nutrients, ready for any financial appetite.

Assessing your portfolio is akin to taking stock of your snack drawer to ensure you have the right mix of flavors and nutrition; it's about striking a balance that aligns with your dietary goals, or in this case, your financial objectives. Regular evaluation of your portfolio composition is crucial to identify any overexposure to certain assets or sectors that might increase your risk or diverge from your investment strategy. Here are some strategies to help you assess your portfolio effectively, ensuring it remains diversified and aligned with your goals.

Establish Clear Investment Goals

Define Objectives: Begin by clarifying your investment goals, risk tolerance, and time horizon. Whether you're aiming for long-term growth, income, or preservation of capital, your objectives will guide your assessment and adjustment strategies.

Analyze Asset Allocation

Current Allocation: Examine the distribution of your investments across different asset classes (cryptocurrencies, stocks, bonds, commodities, real estate, etc.). Does this allocation reflect your risk tolerance and investment goals?

Sector Diversification: Within each asset class, especially cryptocurrencies and stocks, look at your exposure to different sectors. Overconcentration in a single sector, such as tech stocks or DeFi tokens, can increase risk.

Perform a Risk Assessment

Identify High-Risk Investments: Highlight assets in your portfolio that carry higher risk, whether due to volatility, regulatory uncertainty, or market speculation. Consider whether the potential rewards justify the risk based on your goals.

Correlation Analysis: Determine how correlated your investments are. Assets that move in tandem increase your portfolio's risk during market downturns. Aim for a mix of assets that react differently to the same market events.

Evaluate Performance

Benchmarking: Compare the performance of your investments against relevant benchmarks. For cryptocurrencies, this might be comparing altcoins to Bitcoin or Ethereum; for stocks, it might be comparing your holdings to a market index like the S&P 500.

Relative Performance: Assess the performance of your investments relative to each other. Underperforming assets might indicate areas of overexposure or sectors that are not aligning with market trends.

Review for Rebalancing

Need for Rebalancing: Based on your analysis, determine if and how your portfolio needs rebalancing. This might involve reducing positions in overrepresented sectors or assets and increasing diversity by investing in underrepresented ones.

Tax Implications: Consider the tax implications of selling assets, especially if held in taxable accounts. Sometimes, strategic rebalancing within tax-advantaged accounts can help manage potential tax liabilities.

Continuous Monitoring and Learning

Stay Informed: Keep abreast of market trends, economic indicators, and emerging sectors. The investment landscape is constantly evolving, and staying informed can help you anticipate shifts that might affect your portfolio.

Adapt and Adjust: Be prepared to adapt your strategy based on changes in your life circumstances, financial goals, or the broader economic environment. Flexibility is key to maintaining a portfolio that continues to meet your needs over time.

Assessing your portfolio is not a one-time task but an ongoing process that plays a critical role in achieving your investment objectives. By regularly evaluating your portfolio's composition, performance, and alignment with your goals, you can make informed decisions to rebalance and optimize, much like curating the perfect mix of snacks for any occasion. This disciplined approach ensures your investments are well-positioned to navigate the market's ups and downs, supporting your financial health and future prosperity.

Rebalancing your investment portfolio is akin to tuning a musical instrument; it's essential to ensure that each note plays harmoniously with the others, maintaining the intended sound or, in this case, the desired asset allocation. Over time, market movements can cause your portfolio to drift from its target allocation, increasing risk or deviating from your investment strategy. Regular rebalancing brings your portfolio back into alignment, much like adjusting the strings to keep a guitar in tune. Here's how and when to rebalance, employing strategies that ensure your portfolio remains attuned to your financial goals.

Setting Regular Intervals

One common rebalancing technique is to set a regular schedule, such as quarterly, semi-annually, or annually. This method simplifies the decision-making process by making rebalancing a routine maintenance task.

Pros: Automates the rebalancing process, reducing the temptation to make emotional or impulsive investment decisions based on market conditions.

Cons: May not account for significant market events that occur between scheduled rebalances, potentially missing opportunities to adjust more responsively to market dynamics.

Threshold-Based Rebalancing

Another approach is to rebalance when an asset class's weight in your portfolio deviates from its target allocation by a predetermined percentage, often set at 5% or 10%.

Pros: More dynamic than calendar-based rebalancing, allowing for adjustments in response to market movements and maintaining closer alignment with your target asset allocation.

Cons: Requires more frequent monitoring of your portfolio and may lead to higher transaction costs from more frequent trades.

Triggering Events

Certain life events or significant market changes can also trigger a need to rebalance:

Life Events: Changes in your financial situation, risk tolerance, or investment goals, such as retirement, receiving a windfall, or a change in income, may necessitate a portfolio review and adjustment.

Market Events: Major market shifts or economic changes, such as a recession, a bull market, or changes in interest rates, can impact your asset allocation and risk exposure, warranting a rebalance.

Rebalancing Strategies

When rebalancing, consider the following strategies to optimize the process:

Tax Efficiency: Be mindful of the tax implications of selling assets, especially in taxable accounts. Utilizing tax-advantaged accounts for rebalancing when possible can help manage your tax liability.

Transaction Costs: Consider the costs associated with rebalancing, including trade commissions and fees. Opting for commission-free trades or rebalancing through new contributions can minimize costs.

Asset Location: Take into account where your assets are held. Rebalancing within retirement accounts can be more flexible due to the absence of immediate tax consequences compared to taxable accounts.

Maintaining Discipline

The key to successful rebalancing is discipline. It's easy to fall in love with outperforming assets and hesitate to trim those positions, but rebalancing requires a commitment to your long-term strategy over short-term gains. It's about sticking to the composition that aligns with your risk tolerance and financial goals, ensuring that no single investment or asset class can disproportionately impact your portfolio's performance.

Rebalancing is an essential tool in the investor's toolkit, helping to manage risk, adhere to your investment strategy, and navigate the complexities of the financial markets with confidence. By employing regular intervals, responding to threshold deviations, or adjusting for triggering events, you can ensure your portfolio remains in harmony with your financial objectives, ready to face the market's ever-changing tune.

Staying informed in the ever-evolving world of investing is akin to a musician keeping up with the latest trends in music, technology, and theory; it's essential for growth, adaptation, and ensuring your "performance" remains relevant and resonant. In the dynamic landscape of investments, where new technologies, economic shifts, and global events can quickly alter the playing field, being well-informed is not just an advantage—it's a necessity. This section emphasizes the importance of staying updated on market trends and innovations, ensuring your portfolio is attuned to the times and poised for continued growth.

The Pulse of the Market

The financial markets are living entities, pulsating with the rhythms of global economies, investor sentiment, and technological advancements. Staying abreast of these changes allows you to anticipate market movements, adapt your strategy, and make informed decisions.

Economic Indicators: Follow key economic indicators such as inflation rates, employment data, and GDP growth. These metrics can provide insight into the overall health of the economy and potential market directions.

Technological Innovations: Blockchain, artificial intelligence, renewable energy, and biotechnology are just a few sectors where innovation can drive significant market shifts. Being aware of breakthroughs and emerging technologies can uncover investment opportunities.

Regulatory Landscape: Changes in regulations can have profound effects on markets. Whether it's new cryptocurrency guidelines, changes in tax laws, or shifts in trade policies, staying informed helps you navigate potential challenges.

Tools for Staying Informed

Leveraging the right tools can streamline the process of keeping up with the vast amount of information available:

Financial News Platforms: Subscribe to reputable financial news outlets and platforms that offer in-depth analysis and timely updates.

Social Media and Forums: Platforms like Twitter, LinkedIn, and specialized forums can provide real-time insights and discussions among investors and experts.

Podcasts and Webinars: Financial podcasts and webinars are excellent resources for gaining deeper understandings of market trends and investment strategies.

Research Reports and Whitepapers: For those looking to dive deeper, research reports and whitepapers from financial institutions and think tanks offer comprehensive analyses of market trends and sectors.

The Importance of Critical Analysis

While staying informed is crucial, it's equally important to approach the information with a critical mind:

Verify Sources: Always consider the source of your information. Look for reputable, unbiased reporting to avoid misinformation.

Contrarian Views: Expose yourself to a variety of viewpoints, including contrarian opinions. This can provide a more rounded perspective and challenge your assumptions.

Analysis Overload: Be wary of analysis paralysis. While staying informed is key, drowning in too much information can be counterproductive. Find a balance that works for you, ensuring that the influx of information informs rather than overwhelms your decision-making process.

Reflecting Innovations in Your Portfolio

As you absorb new information and insights, periodically review your portfolio to see if adjustments are needed to reflect the changing landscape. This might involve reallocating assets, exploring new sectors, or rebalancing to maintain your desired risk level.

Staying informed is an ongoing process that requires dedication, curiosity, and a commitment to your financial education. It empowers you to navigate the investment landscape with confidence, ensuring your portfolio not only reflects the current market environment but is also poised to capitalize on future opportunities. Just as a musician practices and adapts to stay relevant, a well-informed investor is better equipped to perform successfully in the ever-changing symphony of the financial markets.

Chapter 8

Riding the Waves

Day Trading Tips and Tricks

Mastering technical analysis in day trading is akin to a surfer reading the ocean waves, understanding when to paddle out and when to ride a wave to shore. It's about interpreting the market's signals through charts, indicators, and patterns, allowing you to make informed decisions on entry and exit points with a zen-like focus. This relaxed approach to technical analysis emphasizes patience, practice, and perspective, transforming what can often be an overwhelming flood of data into a stream of actionable insights. Let's break down the essentials of achieving mastery in technical analysis for day trading.

Understanding Chart Types

Candlestick Charts: The foundation of technical analysis, candlestick charts provide a visual representation of price movements within specific time frames, revealing patterns and trends that can guide trading decisions. Learning to read candlestick patterns is like understanding a language, where each formation tells a story about market sentiment and potential moves.

Volume Charts: Volume is a critical indicator of the strength behind price movements. Charts that include volume bars beneath the price action offer clues about the conviction of traders during uptrends or downtrends, much like the volume of a song can indicate the intensity of a musical piece.

Key Technical Indicators

Moving Averages (MA): Moving averages smooth out price data to identify trends. The crossover of short-term and long-term MAs can signal potential entry or exit points, akin to a change in rhythm that prompts a new dance move.

Relative Strength Index (RSI): The RSI measures the speed and change of price movements, indicating overbought or oversold conditions. It's a tool to gauge the market's momentum, helping to time trades more effectively.

MACD (Moving Average Convergence Divergence): This indicator helps identify trend direction and reversals through the relationship between two moving averages of a cryptocurrency's price. Understanding MACD is like syncing to a beat, ensuring your moves align with the market's tempo.

Spotting Patterns

Trend Patterns: Recognize the significance of uptrends, downtrends, and sideways trends. Identifying these can help you understand the market's general direction, much like distinguishing between different genres in music.

Reversal Patterns: Patterns like head and shoulders, double tops, and double bottoms signal potential reversals in the current trend. Spotting these patterns early can help you anticipate shifts, preparing you to adjust your position accordingly.

Continuation Patterns: Flags, pennants, and triangles suggest that the current trend is likely to continue after a brief pause. These patterns can indicate moments to hold your position or prepare for a trade, akin to the anticipation built up during a musical bridge before returning to the chorus.

A Relaxed Approach to Analysis

Patience is Key: Just as not every wave is worth riding, not every market signal warrants action. Cultivate patience to wait for clear, high-probability setups.

Keep a Clear Head: Incorporate mindfulness and stress-reduction techniques to maintain focus and clarity, preventing emotions from clouding your analysis.

Continuous Learning: Technical analysis is a skill honed over time. Commit to lifelong learning, experimenting with different indicators and patterns to find what resonates with your trading style.

Mastering technical analysis for day trading is a journey of developing an intimate understanding of market movements and the ability to interpret these movements calmly and confidently. By approaching analysis with patience, practice, and a zen-like focus, you can navigate the markets with the precision of a skilled surfer, catching waves of opportunity while avoiding the turbulence of unnecessary risk.

In the world of day trading, where the market's waves are ridden with a blend of anticipation and caution, the strategy of low-risk position sizing emerges as a crucial navigational tool. This approach to managing risk through strategic position sizing ensures that the impact of any single trade on your overall portfolio is minimized, much like how a balanced diet keeps any single food from overwhelming your nutritional intake. Let's explore the importance of low-risk position sizing and how it can protect your portfolio from the volatility and unpredictability inherent in day trading.

Understanding Position Sizing

Position sizing refers to the amount of capital allocated to any single trade within your portfolio. The goal is to determine the optimal size that maximizes potential returns while minimizing potential losses, ensuring no single trade can cause significant damage to your overall financial health.

The Role of Risk Management

At the heart of low-risk position sizing is the principle of risk management. By deciding in advance the maximum percentage of your portfolio you are willing to risk on a trade, you create a safety net that guards against the temptation to overcommit based on emotion or overconfidence.

Percentage-Based Risk Management: A common approach is to risk only a small percentage of your total portfolio on any single trade, typically between 1% and 2%. For example, if your portfolio is $10,000, a 1% risk rule means you would not risk more than $100 on a single trade.

Dollar Amount Risk Management: Alternatively, some traders set a fixed dollar amount as their risk limit for each trade, which can vary based on the trader's risk tolerance and portfolio size.

Calculating Position Size

To calculate the position size that aligns with your risk management strategy, you'll need to consider three key factors: your total capital, the risk level per trade (in percentage or dollar amount), and the stop-loss level.

Stop-Loss Orders: Setting a stop-loss order determines the maximum amount you're willing to lose on a trade if the market moves against you. Your position size is then calculated so that if your stop-loss is triggered, you only lose the predetermined amount or percentage of your portfolio.

Position Size Formula: The basic formula for position sizing is: Position Size = Risk Amount / (Entry Price - Stop-Loss Price). This calculation ensures that your risk per trade is kept within your set parameters, protecting your portfolio from significant losses.

The Benefits of Low-Risk Position Sizing

Emotional Equilibrium: By limiting the risk on each trade, traders can maintain a more balanced emotional state, reducing the fear of significant losses and the greed that can lead to overexposure.

Portfolio Longevity: Consistent application of low-risk position sizing ensures that your portfolio can withstand the inevitable losses that come with trading, providing the longevity needed to capitalize on winning trades over time.

Adaptability: This approach allows traders to remain flexible and adjust their strategies based on changing market conditions and personal financial goals without the added pressure of recovering from large losses.

Staying Disciplined

The key to successful low-risk position sizing is discipline. It requires sticking to your predetermined risk management rules, even in the face of enticing market opportunities or after a streak of losses. Much like maintaining a healthy lifestyle involves disciplined eating and exercise habits, protecting your portfolio through low-risk position sizing demands consistency and self-control.

By embracing low-risk position sizing, traders can ride the market's waves with confidence, secure in the knowledge that their navigational strategy is designed to safeguard their portfolio's health, allowing them to explore the vast ocean of day trading opportunities without fear of capsizing.

Having a clear trading plan is like setting up a map before embarking on a road trip; it outlines your destination, the route you plan to take, and the provisions you need. In the context of day trading, this plan includes predefined goals, entry and exit criteria, and risk management strategies. A well-crafted trading plan acts as a beacon, guiding you through the tumultuous seas of the market, ensuring that you make decisions based on logic and strategy rather than emotion or impulse. Let's delve into the significance of setting and sticking to your trading plan and how it can safeguard your journey in the cryptocurrency trading space.

The Foundation of a Trading Plan

Define Your Goals: Start with clear, achievable goals. Are you trading for short-term gains, to supplement income, or as part of a broader investment strategy? Defining what success looks like for you sets the stage for all subsequent decisions.

Entry and Exit Criteria: Specify the conditions that must be met before you enter or exit a trade. This could include technical indicators, price levels, or news events. Having these criteria in place helps eliminate hesitation and second-guessing.

Risk Management: Determine in advance how much of your portfolio you are willing to risk on a single trade and stick to it. This includes setting stop-loss orders to minimize potential losses.

The Role of Discipline

Avoiding Emotional Trading: Emotions can cloud judgment, leading to impulsive decisions like chasing losses or getting greedy. A trading plan serves as a contract with yourself, keeping you disciplined and focused on your strategy rather than your emotions.

Consistency Over Luck: Success in trading comes from making consistently good decisions over time, not from a few lucky trades. Adhering to a well-thought-out trading plan ensures that every move you make is deliberate and aligned with your long-term objectives.

Regular Review and Adaptation

Reflect and Adjust: The cryptocurrency market is dynamic, with conditions that can change rapidly. Regularly review your trading plan to ensure it remains relevant and effective. Be prepared to adjust your strategies based on new information or if your financial situation or goals change.

Learning from Experience: Use your trading journal to track the performance of your trades against your plan. Analyze both your successes and failures to identify what works and what doesn't, refining your plan over time.

Practical Steps to Stick to Your Trading Plan

Checklists: Create checklists based on your trading plan to use before entering and exiting trades. This helps ensure that all criteria are met and that you're not deviating from your plan.

Limitations on Trading Activity: Set limits on how many trades you can make in a day or week to prevent overtrading, a common pitfall that can lead to decision fatigue and increased risk.

Time for Reflection: Allocate time at the end of each trading session to review your actions against your plan. Reflecting on your decision-making process helps reinforce discipline and the habit of following your plan.

Having and sticking to a trading plan is essential for navigating the complexities and volatilities of day trading in the cryptocurrency market. It provides a framework for making informed decisions, minimizes the impact of emotions on trading, and promotes a disciplined approach to achieving your financial goals. Like a map on a road trip, your trading plan is your guide, ensuring that each decision moves you closer to your desired destination, not further away.

In the vast and often wild frontier of cryptocurrency trading, scams lurk around every corner, ready to trip up even the most savvy investors. Much like discerning a mirage from an oasis in a desert, identifying the red flags of common scams can save you from financial peril. This section is dedicated to arming traders with the knowledge to spot these deceptions and navigate safely through the treacherous terrain of the crypto market. Let's explore the hallmarks of typical scams and the strategies to sidestep these traps.

Pump-and-Dump Schemes

Red Flags:

Unsolicited Promotions: Be wary of unexpected social media messages, emails, or forum posts promoting a particular coin or token, claiming it's the next big thing.

Sudden Price Spikes: A rapid increase in price without any corresponding news or development within the project could indicate artificial inflation.

High Volume, Low Market Cap: A mismatch between high trading volume and a low market cap can be a telltale sign of manipulation.

Avoidance Strategies:

Research Before Investing: Always conduct thorough research into a cryptocurrency's fundamentals, team, and market position before investing.

Question the Hype: Approach overly positive promotion with skepticism, especially if the source is anonymous or unverified.

Phishing Attempts

Red Flags:

Suspicious Links: Emails or messages that include links to websites asking for your private keys or wallet passwords.

Impersonation: Communications pretending to be from legitimate companies or entities, often with slight variations in the email address or domain name.

Urgency and Threats: Messages that create a sense of urgency, claiming your account is at risk or that immediate action is required to secure your assets.

Avoidance Strategies:

Verify Sources: Double-check the authenticity of any communication by contacting the company through official channels.

Protect Your Information: Never share your private keys, seed phrases, or passwords, and be cautious about where you enter this information online.

Use Security Software: Employ reputable antivirus and anti-phishing software to help detect and block suspicious activities.

Investment and ICO Scams

Red Flags:

Guaranteed Returns: Promises of guaranteed returns or claims of no risk are major red flags, as all investments carry some level of risk.

Opaque Project Details: Projects that provide vague or minimal information about their objectives, technology, or team.

Pressure to Invest Quickly: Scams often create a false sense of scarcity or time limitation to pressure investors into making quick, uninformed decisions.

Avoidance Strategies:

Diligent Research: Take the time to thoroughly investigate the project, including reading the whitepaper, researching the team members, and checking for legitimate partnerships.

Seek Community Feedback: Look for reviews and feedback from the cryptocurrency community in forums, social media, or reputable news sources.

Be Patient: Resist the urge to invest under pressure. Taking the time to make a well-informed decision is key to avoiding scams.

Social Media and Messaging Scams

Red Flags:

Fake Profiles: Scammers often create fake profiles imitating well-known figures or organizations in the crypto space.

Giveaway Scams: Posts claiming to multiply cryptocurrency sent to a specified wallet address as part of a giveaway or contest.

Direct Message Scams: Unsolicited advice or investment opportunities sent via direct messages.

Avoidance Strategies:

Verify Identities: Check the official websites or verified social media accounts of individuals or organizations to verify the legitimacy of profiles and offers.

Ignore Unsolicited Offers: Treat any unsolicited investment advice or giveaway offers with extreme caution and skepticism.

By staying vigilant and informed, you can spot the red flags of common cryptocurrency scams and protect your investments from predators lurking in the digital landscape. Remember, if an opportunity seems too good to be true, it probably is. Armed with knowledge and caution, you can navigate the crypto markets safely, keeping your assets secure and your trading journey on track.

Overcoming FOMO (Fear of Missing Out) in the cryptocurrency market is akin to resisting the urge to jump onto a departing train, trusting that another will come along that's headed in a direction more aligned with your destination. FOMO can lead traders to make impulsive, often ill-advised decisions, driven by hype, buzz, or the fear of missing out on potential profits. This section explores the psychological underpinnings of FOMO and provides strategies to navigate the crypto markets with a calm, focused mindset, ensuring decisions are made on a rational rather than emotional basis.

Understanding FOMO

FOMO is a psychological response triggered by seeing others experience or gain something, stirring a fear of being left out. In crypto trading, it's often fueled by rapid price increases, social media hype, or sensational news stories, prompting a fear-driven rush into investments without proper analysis or consideration of risk.

Strategies to Combat FOMO

Establish and Trust Your Trading Plan

Clarity on Goals: Clearly defined trading goals and strategies act as your north star, guiding decisions based on your financial objectives and risk tolerance, rather than the market's mood swings.

Discipline in Execution: Commit to your trading plan, resisting the temptation to deviate based on the market's euphoria. Remember, successful trading is a marathon, not a sprint.

Stay Informed but Filter the Noise

Selective Consumption: Stay updated on market trends and news, but be selective in your sources. Seek information that offers analysis and insights, rather than sensationalism or hype.

Critical Analysis: Approach what you read and hear with a critical mind. Question the motives behind overly bullish or bearish sentiments and consider multiple viewpoints before forming your opinion.

Practice Mindfulness and Emotional Awareness

Mindfulness Exercises: Regular mindfulness practices can help you recognize and acknowledge your emotional responses without being controlled by them. Techniques like meditation or deep breathing can center your thoughts and reduce impulsivity.

Emotional Check-ins: Regularly assess your emotional state before making trading decisions. If you detect anxiety, excitement, or fear driving your actions, take a step back to reevaluate.

Diversify Your Portfolio

Spread the Risk: Diversification across different assets and sectors can alleviate the pressure to hit on every market opportunity. Knowing your investments are spread out can provide peace of mind and reduce the impulse to chase every rising star.

Learn from Past Experiences

Reflect on Misses and Hits: Analyze instances where FOMO influenced your decisions. Assess the outcomes to understand the real impact of those choices, integrating these lessons into future decision-making processes.

Foster a Community of Rational Traders

Supportive Networks: Engage with a community of traders who emphasize rational, informed decision-making. Sharing experiences and strategies can offer perspective and reduce the sense of isolation that sometimes fuels FOMO.

Acceptance

Embrace Missed Opportunities: Acknowledge that missing out is inevitable and not inherently negative. Each decision not to invest is also a decision to avoid potential loss, emphasizing the importance of choice in trading.

Combating FOMO is not about eliminating fear but managing and mitigating its influence on your trading decisions. By fostering discipline, mindfulness, and a commitment to your trading plan, you can navigate the crypto markets with confidence and clarity, making decisions that align with your long-term goals rather than the fleeting winds of market hype. In doing so, you ensure that your trading journey is defined by thoughtful strategy rather than the fear of missing out.

Emotional discipline in the realm of day trading is akin to a seasoned sailor remaining calm and composed amidst turbulent seas. The cryptocurrency market, with its inherent volatility, can provoke a whirlwind of emotional reactions, from the thrill of a surge to the despair of a dip. Managing these emotional reactions is crucial, as they can cloud judgment, leading to hasty decisions and potential missteps. This section delves into techniques for cultivating emotional discipline, emphasizing detachment and the maintenance of a cool head amid market uncertainty.

Recognizing Emotional Triggers

Self-Awareness: The first step in emotional discipline is recognizing your emotional triggers. Keep a trading journal that not only records trades but also notes the emotions you felt at the time. Over time, patterns will emerge, highlighting specific market conditions or outcomes that trigger emotional responses.

Establishing a Routine

Pre-Trade Rituals: Establish rituals before you begin trading each day to center yourself. This might involve meditation, a review of your trading plan, or a physical warm-up. A consistent routine can help shift your mindset to a more analytical and less emotional state.

Setting Clear Rules

Automate Decision-Making: Where possible, use tools like stop-loss orders and automated trading systems to make decisions based on predefined criteria rather than in-the-moment emotions. Automation can act as a guardrail, keeping your trading strategy on track.

Risk Management: Clearly define your risk for each trade and overall. Knowing you have a cap on potential losses can alleviate the anxiety of market swings.

Practicing Mindfulness and Stress Reduction

Mindfulness Meditation: Regular practice of mindfulness meditation can enhance your ability to observe thoughts and emotions without being swept away by them. This detachment is invaluable for maintaining clarity and composure in decision-making.

Physical Exercise: Incorporate physical activity into your daily routine. Exercise is a powerful stress reliever and can help maintain emotional equilibrium.

Fostering Emotional Resilience

Educate and Prepare: Understand that volatility is a characteristic of the crypto market, not a deviation from the norm. Educating yourself about market cycles and historical trends can prepare you mentally for the ups and downs, reducing the shock and emotional impact of sudden movements.

Reflective Practice: Regularly review your trading performance, including both successes and failures. Reflection helps you learn from experience and gradually reduces the emotional weight of individual trades.

Developing a Support System

Community Engagement: Connect with a community of fellow traders. Sharing experiences and strategies can provide emotional support and perspective, reminding you that you're not alone in navigating the market's challenges.

Embracing Detachment

Psychological Detachment: Cultivate an attitude of detachment towards both profits and losses. View trading as a performance, where the focus is on executing your strategy to the best of your ability, rather than on the outcome of any single trade.

Balanced Life Perspective: Ensure that trading is just one aspect of a well-rounded life. Engaging in hobbies, spending time with loved ones, and pursuing personal goals can provide a healthy balance, reducing the emotional weight attached to trading outcomes.

Emotional discipline is not about suppressing emotions but managing them in a way that they do not dictate your trading decisions. By implementing these techniques, traders can navigate the crypto market's volatility with a level head and clear focus, making informed decisions based on strategy rather than fleeting feelings. This disciplined approach not only enhances trading performance but also contributes to overall well-being, allowing traders to ride the market's waves with confidence and equanimity.

Continuous learning and adaptation in day trading are akin to a musician mastering their craft; just as musical genres evolve and new instruments emerge, so too does the landscape of the cryptocurrency market. The importance of staying abreast of market trends, technological advancements, and regulatory changes cannot be overstated. This constant flow of new information can significantly impact trading strategies and outcomes. Engaging in ongoing education and staying informed is crucial for making well-informed decisions that align with the current state of the market. Let's delve into why continuous learning is pivotal and how it can be seamlessly integrated into your trading routine.

The Dynamism of the Crypto Market

The cryptocurrency market is characterized by rapid changes and innovations. New cryptocurrencies, technologies like blockchain enhancements, and DeFi platforms are continually emerging. Each of these can introduce new opportunities and risks to traders. Additionally, the regulatory environment surrounding cryptocurrencies is still evolving, with new policies and guidelines that can greatly impact market dynamics.

Strategies for Continuous Learning

Utilize a Variety of Resources

Financial News Platforms: Subscribe to reputable financial news outlets that specialize in cryptocurrencies and blockchain technology to get timely updates on market movements and tech innovations.

Online Courses and Webinars: Take advantage of the myriad of online courses, webinars, and workshops available on cryptocurrency trading and blockchain technology. Many of these resources are available for free or at a nominal cost.

Follow Thought Leaders and Communities

Social Media and Forums: Platforms like Twitter, Reddit, and specialized crypto forums host vibrant communities where traders share insights, strategies, and the latest news. Following thought leaders and participating in these communities can provide valuable information and diverse perspectives.

Podcasts and YouTube Channels: Many experts share their knowledge through podcasts and YouTube channels, offering analyses of current market trends, technological advancements, and trading strategies.

Understand Regulatory Changes

Government and Regulatory Websites: Regularly check websites of financial regulatory bodies for updates on cryptocurrency regulations. Understanding the legal landscape is crucial for compliance and can offer insight into market directions.

Embrace Experimentation

Paper Trading: Use simulation trading platforms to experiment with new strategies without financial risk. This hands-on approach to learning can deepen your understanding of market dynamics and the practical application of your knowledge.

The Importance of Adaptation

Review and Adjust Your Strategies: As you acquire new knowledge, regularly review and adjust your trading strategies to reflect the latest market conditions and technologies. What worked yesterday may not work tomorrow in the fast-paced crypto market.

Openness to Change: Cultivate an openness to change, recognizing that adaptation is a key component of long-term success in trading. Flexibility in your approach allows you to pivot as the market evolves.

Continuous learning and adaptation are the hallmarks of a successful day trader. By committing to ongoing education and staying informed about market trends, technological advancements, and regulatory changes, you equip yourself with the tools necessary to navigate the complexities of the cryptocurrency market. This proactive approach ensures that your trading strategies remain relevant, robust, and responsive to the dynamic trading environment, helping you to capitalize on opportunities and mitigate risks.

In the high-stakes arena of day trading, where stress levels can soar and focus is paramount, integrating mindfulness and meditation into your routine can be transformative. These practices, tailored for traders, are not just about seeking a moment of tranquility; they're about honing your mental edge, enhancing decision-making capabilities, and fostering a state of calm awareness amidst the market's tumult. Mindfulness and meditation can help traders navigate the emotional highs and lows of trading, ensuring that each decision is grounded in clarity rather than clouded by impulse. Let's explore specific exercises and techniques designed to benefit traders.

Starting with Mindfulness

Mindfulness is the practice of being fully present and engaged in the moment, aware of your thoughts and feelings without distraction or judgment. For traders, this can translate to an increased awareness of their mental state and a more deliberate approach to trading decisions.

Mindful Breathing: Begin with simple mindful breathing exercises. Sit comfortably, close your eyes, and focus solely on your breath. Notice the sensation of air entering and leaving your body. This practice can help center your thoughts and reduce stress, creating mental clarity for the trading day ahead.

Mindful Observation: Choose an object in your vicinity and focus all your attention on it for a minute or two. Observe it without judgment, noting its colors, shapes, and other characteristics. This exercise trains your mind to focus on the present, reducing the impact of distracting or anxious thoughts.

Meditation Techniques for Traders

Meditation builds on mindfulness, offering techniques to deepen your sense of calm and improve concentration. Even a few minutes a day can significantly impact stress levels and cognitive function.

Guided Meditation: There are many apps and online resources offering guided meditations tailored to different needs, including stress reduction, focus enhancement, and emotional balance. Starting with guided sessions can help ease you into a consistent meditation practice.

Visualization Meditation: Visualization is a powerful tool for traders. Visualize successful trades, imagine navigating challenging market conditions with ease, or picture yourself achieving your trading goals. This positive imagery can boost confidence and reduce anxiety.

Integrating Mindfulness into Trading

Mindful Trading Routine: Incorporate brief mindfulness exercises before you begin trading and during breaks. Taking a moment to center yourself can help maintain emotional equilibrium throughout the trading day.

Awareness of Emotional States: Use mindfulness to become more aware of your emotional state while trading. Recognizing feelings of stress, excitement, or frustration early on allows you to address them before they influence your trading decisions.

The Benefits of Regular Practice

Reduced Stress: Regular mindfulness and meditation can lower stress levels, not just during trading hours but in general life, promoting overall well-being.

Enhanced Decision-Making: By improving focus and reducing emotional reactivity, mindfulness and meditation can lead to better trading decisions, helping to avoid impulsive actions based on fear or greed.

Increased Discipline: These practices foster a greater sense of discipline, both in sticking to your trading plan and in your overall approach to the markets.

Conclusion

Incorporating mindfulness and meditation into your daily routine offers a sanctuary of calm in the high-energy world of day trading. These practices not only enhance mental and emotional well-being but also sharpen the cognitive skills essential for success in the markets. By fostering a state of focused calm, traders can navigate the complexities of day trading with enhanced clarity, resilience, and precision, turning the act of trading into a practice of mindfulness itself.

Creating a supportive trading environment is about more than just having a comfortable chair or a spacious desk; it's about cultivating a space that promotes calmness, concentration, and well-being, enabling you to approach trading with a clear mind and a focused demeanor. Just as a serene and well-organized studio inspires an artist, a thoughtfully arranged trading space can significantly enhance your ability to make informed, deliberate decisions under pressure. Here are some key considerations and advice for setting up a trading environment that supports your success.

Ergonomic Comfort

Adjustable Chair and Desk: Invest in a high-quality chair and desk with adjustable features to support a comfortable posture over long trading sessions. Ergonomic comfort reduces physical strain, which in turn minimizes stress and fatigue.

Monitor Height and Distance: Position your monitor(s) at eye level and at a comfortable viewing distance to avoid straining your neck and eyes. This can help maintain focus and reduce headaches or eye strain.

Calming Aesthetics

Natural Light: If possible, set up your trading space near a source of natural light. Sunlight can boost your mood and energy levels. When natural light isn't available, choose lighting that mimics daylight to help maintain your circadian rhythm.

Plants: Incorporating greenery into your trading space can have a calming effect, improve air quality, and enhance your connection to the natural world, providing a peaceful backdrop to the digital arena of trading.

Minimalist Setup

Clutter-Free Desk: Keep your trading area clean and uncluttered. A minimalist setup helps reduce distractions, allowing you to focus on the task at hand. Regularly organize your space to keep it conducive to concentration.

Organized Tools: Have all necessary trading tools and resources within easy reach but avoid overcrowding your workspace. This includes trading journals, charts, and any software or hardware you use regularly.

Personal Comforts

Personalize Your Space: Add personal touches that make the space uniquely yours and evoke a sense of calm, such as photos, art, or motivational quotes. These elements can serve as reminders of your trading goals and personal motivations.

Comfort Items: Consider adding a few comfort items to your trading environment, such as a high-quality pair of headphones for listening to calming music or ambient sounds, a stress ball, or an aromatherapy diffuser with soothing scents like lavender or peppermint.

Technology Setup

Reliable Hardware and Software: Ensure your computer and internet connection are reliable and fast enough to handle real-time trading without delays. Technical disruptions can cause unnecessary stress and potentially impact trading decisions.

Backup Solutions: Have backup solutions in place, such as a secondary internet connection or power source, to mitigate the stress of technical failures.

Quiet and Privacy

Dedicated Space: If possible, dedicate a room or a defined area solely for trading. This separation from household distractions can help you enter a focused trading mindset.

Sound Management: Consider soundproofing solutions or use noise-canceling headphones to minimize disruptive noise, allowing you to maintain concentration during critical trading moments.

Creating a supportive trading environment is an investment in your overall trading performance and well-being. By ensuring your physical comfort, fostering a calm and focused atmosphere, and personalizing your space to reflect your preferences, you set the stage for a more disciplined, mindful, and ultimately successful trading practice.

Chapter 9

Beyond the Smoke

Growing as a Trader

In the vast and often overwhelming world of cryptocurrency trading, where information abounds and new content is constantly generated, the art of curated learning becomes invaluable. This approach is about prioritizing quality over quantity, honing the skill to sift through the noise to find information that truly adds value to your trading knowledge and skills. Like a discerning collector who carefully selects each piece for their gallery, a trader must learn to select learning materials that enrich their understanding without cluttering their mind. Let's explore strategies for curated learning in the context of cryptocurrency trading.

Identify Reputable Sources

Start by identifying sources known for their credibility and depth of analysis. Look for authors, analysts, and platforms recognized for their expertise and contributions to the crypto community. Prioritize sources that offer:

In-depth Analysis: Choose materials that provide thorough examination over superficial coverage. Depth involves exploring the historical context, potential future implications, and the technical underpinnings of topics.

Evidence-Based Information: Focus on content supported by data, research, and sound reasoning. Reliable sources typically cite their references, allowing you to explore the information further if desired.

Utilize Curated Platforms

Leverage platforms and services that curate content for you. Many platforms aggregate news, research papers, and educational content, filtering it based on relevance and quality. Utilizing these can save time and ensure you're exposed to high-quality information.

News Aggregators: Use news aggregators tailored for crypto markets to stay updated on the latest developments without having to scour multiple sources.

Educational Platforms: Platforms offering curated courses or webinars can provide structured learning paths, making it easier to dive deep into specific areas of interest.

Develop Critical Thinking Skills

Curated learning isn't just about finding good sources; it's also about approaching information with a critical mindset. Developing critical thinking skills enables you to assess the value and bias of the information you encounter.

Question Motives and Bias: Consider why the information was published and whether the source has any biases that could color the presentation of facts.

Cross-Reference Information: Don't rely on a single source for your learning. Cross-reference facts and viewpoints to get a fuller picture of the topic at hand.

Engage with Communities

Participating in communities can be a form of curated learning, as discussions and debates can highlight valuable resources and new perspectives.

Forums and Social Media: Engage with crypto trading communities on platforms like Reddit, Twitter, and specialized forums. The collective wisdom and experience of a community can direct you to valuable learning resources.

Study Groups: Join or form study groups with fellow traders. These groups can share and discuss resources, providing a collective filter for quality.

Schedule Regular Reviews

Information and market dynamics evolve. What's relevant today may be outdated tomorrow. Schedule regular reviews of your learning materials and sources to ensure they remain current and valuable.

Update Your Resources: As you grow in your trading journey, your learning needs will change. Periodically reassess and update your resources to match your current learning goals.

Reflect on Learning: Take time to reflect on what you've learned and how it applies to your trading strategy. This reflection can help cement your knowledge and identify areas needing further exploration.

Curated learning is a dynamic and ongoing process that emphasizes quality and relevance, ensuring that your educational efforts directly contribute to your growth as a trader. By carefully selecting and critically engaging with information, you can build a solid foundation of knowledge that supports informed decision-making and continuous improvement in the fast-paced world of cryptocurrency trading.

In the relentless rhythm of the cryptocurrency markets, where the tempo never slows and the melody is ever-changing, the importance of scheduled breaks cannot be overstated. Just as a musician must rest their fingers and their mind between sets, traders need to step away from screen time and market monitoring to maintain their performance and prevent burnout. This section not only highlights the necessity of regular breaks but also offers guidance on recognizing the signs of burnout and strategies for effective recovery.

The Necessity of Scheduled Breaks

Continuous engagement with the markets, especially in a landscape as volatile as cryptocurrency, can lead to decision fatigue, reduced concentration, and, ultimately, burnout. Scheduled breaks serve several critical functions:

Mental Clarity: Just as a brief intermission allows an audience to absorb a performance, stepping away from the markets can help clear your mind, allowing for better decision-making upon your return.

Stress Reduction: Regular breaks reduce stress by providing a mental and emotional respite from the constant pressure of trading.

Physical Health: Taking time to move and step away from your desk combats the physical strain of prolonged sitting and screen exposure.

Recognizing Signs of Burnout

Burnout creeps in quietly but has profound effects. Key indicators include:

Chronic Fatigue: Feeling tired not just physically, but mentally exhausted, as if your cognitive resources are depleted.

Diminished Interest: A sense of detachment or lack of enthusiasm for trading, markets, and activities that previously excited you.

Irritability and Frustration: Minor setbacks or challenges evoke disproportionate feelings of irritation or frustration.

Cognitive Difficulties: Experiencing trouble focusing, remembering details, or making decisions.

Strategies for Taking Effective Breaks

Schedule Regularly

Timed Breaks: Integrate breaks into your trading schedule. Use tools or apps to remind you to take short breaks every hour for a few minutes and longer breaks every few hours to disconnect completely.

Engage in Different Activities

Physical Exercise: Engage in physical activity, whether it's a short walk, stretching, or a workout. Physical movement not only counters the sedentary nature of trading but also helps reduce stress.

Mindfulness Practices: Short meditation or breathing exercises during breaks can help reset your mental state.

Hobbies: Spend break time on non-trading related hobbies or interests, providing a complete mental shift from the markets.

Strategies for Recovery from Burnout

Step Back

Take a Temporary Break: If signs of burnout are evident, consider taking a more extended break from trading. Use this time to recuperate, reflect, and reassess your approach to trading.

Reassess Your Strategy

Review Trading Plan: Use the time away to review your trading plan and strategies. Burnout can often signal misalignment between your trading practices and your goals or risk tolerance.

Seek Support

Community and Social Support: Engage with fellow traders, friends, or family. Sharing experiences and challenges can provide emotional relief and valuable perspectives.

Professional Help

Consult a Professional: If burnout significantly impacts your life, consulting a mental health professional can provide strategies for coping and recovery.

Scheduled breaks and mindful recognition of burnout signs are essential practices for sustaining a long-term career in cryptocurrency trading. By integrating these practices into your trading routine, you ensure that you remain sharp, focused, and, most importantly, healthy, both mentally and physically, allowing you to enjoy the symphony of the markets without being overwhelmed by its intensity.

Integrating mindfulness and well-being practices into the life of a trader is akin to adding layers of harmony to the complex melody of trading. These practices support not only mental and physical health but also enhance trading performance by fostering a balanced, focused state of mind. In the high-stakes world of cryptocurrency trading, where stress can be a constant companion, mindfulness, exercise, and engaging in hobbies become essential components of a successful trader's routine. Let's explore how these practices can be woven into the fabric of daily life, offering traders a sanctuary of calm and strength amidst market turbulence.

Mindfulness Practices

Mindfulness involves being fully present and engaged with the current moment, without judgment. For traders, this can translate to an improved ability to make decisions under pressure and a decrease in reactive emotional trading.

Daily Meditation: Starting or ending your day with meditation can help center your thoughts, reduce anxiety, and improve concentration. Even a few minutes can make a significant difference.

Breathing Exercises: Incorporate short breathing exercises throughout your trading day, especially during moments of high stress or decision-making. Techniques like the 4-7-8 breath (inhale for 4 seconds, hold for 7 seconds, exhale for 8 seconds) can quickly restore a sense of calm.

Physical Exercise

Regular physical activity is crucial for maintaining health, reducing stress, and improving cognitive function, all of which are beneficial for trading.

Routine Exercise: Incorporate regular exercise into your routine, whether it's a morning jog, yoga, strength training, or any activity that you enjoy and gets you moving. Exercise not only keeps the body healthy but also clears the mind and boosts mood.

Active Breaks: During your trading day, take active breaks to stretch or do some light exercise. This helps reduce the physical and mental strain of long periods of sitting and screen time.

Hobbies Outside of Trading

Engaging in hobbies and interests outside of trading can provide a much-needed counterbalance to the intensity of the markets, fostering a well-rounded life.

Creative Outlets: Pursue creative hobbies like painting, music, writing, or cooking. Creative activities can be particularly therapeutic, offering a form of expression and distraction from the analytical focus of trading.

Outdoor Activities: Spend time in nature, whether it's hiking, gardening, or simply taking walks. The natural environment has a calming effect, reducing stress and promoting mental clarity.

Social Activities: Make time for social activities and nurturing relationships. Social interaction is crucial for emotional well-being and can provide a support network outside the volatility of the markets.

Integrating Well-being into Your Trading Routine

Schedule: Just as you schedule your trading activities, set specific times for mindfulness practices, exercise, and hobbies. Treating these activities as non-negotiable appointments ensures they are a consistent part of your routine.

Mindful Trading: Apply mindfulness to your trading practice. Before making a trade, take a moment to assess your emotional state, ensuring decisions are made based on analysis and strategy rather than impulse or emotion.

Reflect: Regularly reflect on the benefits these practices bring to your trading and overall quality of life. This reflection can reinforce their value, encouraging their continuation.

Incorporating mindfulness, exercise, and hobbies into the life of a trader is not a luxury but a necessity for sustained success and well-being. These practices create a foundation of mental and physical health that supports peak performance in trading and a fulfilling life beyond the markets. By prioritizing well-being, traders can navigate the complexities of the cryptocurrency market with resilience, clarity, and a deep sense of balance.

Community engagement stands as a beacon for traders navigating the often solitary and tumultuous waters of cryptocurrency trading. Engaging with online forums, social media groups, and attending conferences or meetups can significantly enhance a trader's journey, providing not just insights and knowledge, but also support and camaraderie. Like musicians sharing and discussing their art, traders can greatly benefit from exchanging ideas, strategies, and experiences with their peers. This section delves into the benefits of such engagement and offers guidance on making the most of these community interactions.

Benefits of Community Engagement

Expanded Knowledge Base

The collective wisdom of a community can cover far more ground than any individual could alone. From technical analysis and market predictions to the latest developments in blockchain technology, engaging with a community keeps you at the forefront of knowledge.

Diverse Perspectives

Communities bring together individuals from various backgrounds, each with their unique viewpoints and experiences. This diversity enriches your understanding and can challenge your assumptions, fostering a more well-rounded approach to trading.

Emotional Support

Trading, especially in the volatile crypto market, can be an emotional rollercoaster. Communities offer a sense of belonging and understanding, providing emotional support through the ups and downs. Sharing successes and setbacks with peers who understand the stakes can be incredibly validating and motivating.

Networking Opportunities

Participation in forums, social media groups, and events opens up numerous networking opportunities. These connections can lead to collaborations, partnerships, or mentorship relationships that further your trading career.

Engaging Positively and Learning from the Community

Be an Active Contributor

Share Knowledge: Don't hesitate to share your insights and experiences. Whether it's a successful trade strategy, an analysis of market trends, or lessons learned from a setback, your contributions can add significant value to the community.

Ask Questions: Asking thoughtful questions not only aids your learning but also stimulates discussion and can bring clarity to others with similar queries.

Practice Respect and Open-mindedness

Respect Diverse Opinions: Approach discussions with respect and openness, valuing different perspectives even when they contradict your own. The goal is not to win an argument but to deepen understanding.

Constructive Feedback: Offer constructive feedback when discussing strategies or ideas. Critique the idea, not the person, fostering a positive and supportive environment.

Leverage Meetups and Conferences

Active Participation: When attending meetups or conferences, actively engage with speakers and participants. These interactions can provide deeper insights and build meaningful connections.

Follow Up: After the event, follow up with individuals you connected with. A quick message or email can solidify the connection and open doors for future interactions.

Digital Etiquette

Mind Your Digital Footprint: Remember that your contributions and interactions online are lasting. Maintain professionalism and courtesy, as these interactions reflect on you as a trader and a community member.

Community engagement is a powerful tool in a trader's arsenal, offering not just learning opportunities but also emotional support and networking avenues. By contributing positively and engaging respectfully, you can maximize the benefits of community interactions, enriching both your trading journey and the collective knowledge of the community. In doing so, you not only grow as a trader but also contribute to the growth and positivity of the trading community at large.

In the dynamic and often complex world of cryptocurrency trading, the role of mentorship can be likened to that of a seasoned guide in a vast, uncharted territory. Whether finding a mentor to illuminate the path or becoming one to share your knowledge and insights, mentorship is a powerful conduit for growth, learning, and support. This section explores the multifaceted value of mentorship in the trading sphere, detailing how it can accelerate the learning process, offer emotional support during turbulent times, and introduce fresh perspectives and strategies.

The Value of Finding a Mentor

Accelerated Learning Curve

A mentor brings years of experience and knowledge, providing shortcuts to learning that can significantly speed up your journey. They can help you navigate common pitfalls, understand complex concepts, and apply strategies that have been proven effective, saving you from costly trial and error.

Emotional Support and Encouragement

Trading can be a solitary and stressful endeavor, especially when faced with setbacks. A mentor acts as a steadfast support system, offering encouragement and understanding derived from their own experiences. This emotional backing can be crucial in maintaining morale and perseverance.

Exposure to New Perspectives

Mentors can introduce you to new ways of thinking and approaches to trading that you may not have considered. Their experience in different markets, with various strategies, and through numerous market cycles, enriches your understanding and opens you to a broader range of tactics and philosophies.

The Rewards of Becoming a Mentor

Giving Back and Contributing

For seasoned traders, becoming a mentor offers the opportunity to give back to the trading community by nurturing the next generation of traders. This contribution not only helps others grow but also strengthens the community and the industry as a whole.

Enhanced Understanding and Skills

Teaching others is one of the most effective ways to deepen your own understanding. Articulating concepts, strategies, and insights to a mentee can clarify your own thoughts and reveal gaps in your knowledge, prompting further learning and growth.

Professional and Personal Fulfillment

Mentorship is rewarding beyond the transfer of knowledge—it's a relationship that can lead to profound professional and personal fulfillment. Watching a mentee succeed, knowing you've played a part in their journey, is immensely satisfying. Additionally, the relationship can evolve into a lasting friendship or professional partnership.

Engaging in Effective Mentorship

Setting Clear Expectations

A successful mentor-mentee relationship is built on clear expectations. Discuss goals, availability, and the scope of guidance to ensure both parties are aligned and committed.

Open Communication and Feedback

Foster an environment where open communication and honest feedback are encouraged. Regular check-ins and discussions about progress, challenges, and adjustments to strategies ensure the mentorship remains beneficial.

Mutual Respect and Learning

While the mentor-mentee relationship may seem one-sided, it's truly reciprocal. Mentors can learn from their mentees' fresh perspectives, questions, and experiences, keeping them connected to the evolving market and new ideas.

Mentorship in cryptocurrency trading is a symbiotic relationship that enriches both mentor and mentee, fostering growth, resilience, and a deeper appreciation of the art of trading. Whether seeking guidance to navigate the complexities of the market or offering your wisdom to help others find their way, mentorship accelerates learning, provides support, and cultivates a richer, more connected trading community.

Collaborative learning in the realm of cryptocurrency trading is like forming a band where each member brings their unique skills and insights, contributing to a richer, more harmonious sound. This approach leverages the collective knowledge, experience, and perspectives of peers to tackle the complexities of the market together. By joining or forming study groups, trading clubs, or engaging in online communities focused on specific aspects of crypto trading, individuals can enhance their learning, gain new insights, and refine their strategies in a supportive environment. Let's explore the avenues for collaborative learning and the benefits it offers to traders.

Joining Study Groups

Study groups provide a structured setting for exploring trading concepts, market analysis, and strategies. These groups can meet regularly to:

Discuss Current Market Trends: Share observations on market movements, exchange interpretations of technical indicators, and debate potential future directions.

Review Trades: Collectively analyze completed trades, offering constructive feedback and identifying lessons learned.

Learn New Concepts: Tackle complex trading concepts or new technologies as a group, allowing members to learn from each other's insights and questions.

Forming Trading Clubs

Trading clubs extend the concept of study groups by incorporating more formalized trading activities, such as collective investment pools or simulated trading competitions. Clubs can:

Host Guest Speakers: Invite experienced traders, financial analysts, or industry professionals to share their knowledge and experiences.

Organize Workshops: Conduct workshops on specific trading tools, software, or analysis methods, facilitating hands-on learning.

Engage in Collaborative Trading: Experiment with collaborative trading strategies in a low-risk environment, such as through paper trading or using a small, shared investment fund.

Engaging in Online Communities

The digital nature of cryptocurrency trading lends itself well to online communities. Platforms like Reddit, Discord, and specialized forums host vibrant groups where traders can:

Share Real-time Insights: Post live updates, news, and analysis, offering immediate access to a wide range of information and interpretations.

Participate in Themed Discussions: Engage in threads or channels focused on particular cryptocurrencies, trading strategies, or market analysis techniques.

Access Global Perspectives: Benefit from the global nature of cryptocurrency markets by gaining insights from traders in different countries and time zones.

Benefits of Collaborative Learning

Diverse Perspectives: Collaboration exposes you to a variety of viewpoints, enhancing your ability to see the market from different angles.

Emotional Support: Trading can be isolating; engaging with peers provides a sense of community and support, especially important during challenging market conditions.

Accelerated Learning: The combined knowledge and experience of a group can significantly speed up the learning process, making complex concepts more accessible.

Accountability: Working within a group can increase your accountability, encouraging consistency in study, analysis, and trading activities.

Tips for Effective Collaboration

Define Goals and Rules: Clearly define the objectives and guidelines of the group to ensure alignment and focus.

Encourage Active Participation: Foster an environment where all members are encouraged to contribute, ensuring a rich exchange of ideas.

Respect Differences: Approach disagreements or debates with respect and openness, recognizing that differing opinions can spark valuable insights.

Collaborative learning in cryptocurrency trading enriches your educational journey, offering a multifaceted understanding of the market while providing support and camaraderie. By actively engaging with peers through study groups, trading clubs, or online communities, traders can navigate the complex and ever-changing landscape of the crypto market with greater confidence, depth of knowledge, and a sense of shared purpose.

Lifestyle design in the context of cryptocurrency trading is about more than the pursuit of financial success; it's about creating a holistic life that balances trading ambitions with personal well-being, relationships, and other interests. This conscious approach to crafting your daily life ensures that trading enriches your existence rather than consuming it. Like a carefully composed piece of music that balances melody, harmony, and rhythm, a well-designed trader's lifestyle harmonizes work, play, and rest. Let's explore how traders can thoughtfully design their lifestyles to support both their trading goals and overall life satisfaction.

Setting Holistic Goals

Begin by setting goals that encompass not only your trading aspirations but also personal growth, health, relationships, and hobbies. Goals should be SMART (Specific, Measurable, Achievable, Relevant, and Time-bound) and reflect what truly matters to you.

Structuring Your Day

Balanced Routine: Structure your day to include dedicated trading time, physical activity, relaxation, and family or social time. Like segments in a day planner, each aspect of your life deserves attention and space.

Flexible Scheduling: Allow for flexibility in your schedule to adapt to market conditions or personal needs. A rigid routine may not suit the unpredictable nature of trading or life's spontaneous moments.

Prioritizing Well-being

Physical Health: Incorporate regular exercise, a nutritious diet, and sufficient sleep into your lifestyle. A healthy body supports a sharp mind, essential for effective trading decisions.

Mental Health: Practice mindfulness or meditation to manage stress and maintain emotional equilibrium. Recognize the signs of burnout and have strategies in place for recovery and self-care.

Cultivating Relationships

Trading can be isolating. Make conscious efforts to maintain and nurture relationships with family and friends.

Quality Time: Schedule uninterrupted time with loved ones, ensuring that your trading does not encroach upon these precious moments.

Open Communication: Share your trading journey with your close ones, discussing both the challenges and successes. This transparency helps build understanding and support.

Pursuing Hobbies and Interests

Engaging in hobbies and interests outside of trading can provide a refreshing counterbalance to the demands of the market.

Creative Outlets: Explore creative pursuits such as art, music, writing, or cooking. Creative activities can offer mental breaks and a sense of accomplishment unrelated to trading.

Learning and Growth: Commit to lifelong learning, whether related to trading or other fields of interest. Continuous learning enriches your life and can even provide new insights into your trading.

Embracing Flexibility and Adaptation

Regular Review: Periodically review your lifestyle design to ensure it remains aligned with your evolving goals and circumstances. Life is dynamic; your lifestyle design should be too.

Adaptation: Be willing to adapt your lifestyle in response to trading outcomes, life changes, or shifts in priorities. Flexibility is key to maintaining harmony between trading and life.

Designing a lifestyle that integrates trading with personal well-being and fulfillment requires intentionality and balance. It's about making conscious choices that align with your values, goals, and what brings you joy. By doing so, you create a life where trading is part of a richer tapestry, filled with growth, relationships, and pursuits that feed your soul and sustain your passion for the markets.

Effective time management for traders is akin to a conductor orchestrating a symphony; each section must come in at the right moment for the performance to harmonize beautifully. For cryptocurrency traders, the challenge lies in balancing the demands of market research and trading with the equally important aspects of life outside the markets. Implementing time management strategies allows for a well-rounded existence, ensuring that trading enriches rather than dominates your life. This section explores strategies to manage time effectively, emphasizing the importance of setting boundaries to safeguard personal time.

Prioritization: The Key to Efficiency

Identify High-Value Activities: Determine which trading activities contribute most significantly to your success, such as market analysis or strategy development, and prioritize these in your schedule.

Allocate Time Wisely: Divide your day into blocks of time dedicated to specific activities, including research, trading, and personal commitments. This structured approach helps ensure that critical tasks receive the attention they deserve.

Setting Boundaries

Trading Hours: Establish fixed hours for trading and research, and stick to them. This not only instills discipline but also helps contain trading activities within a designated part of your day, leaving room for other aspects of life.

Digital Detox: Schedule regular intervals where you disconnect from digital devices and online platforms, particularly those related to trading. This can help reduce stress and prevent burnout.

The Art of Saying No

Guard Your Time: Learn to decline activities or commitments that don't align with your priorities or contribute to your goals. Saying no is essential for maintaining focus and ensuring your time is spent on what truly matters.

Utilizing Technology for Efficiency

Automation Tools: Leverage technology to automate routine trading tasks where possible, such as using trading bots for specific strategies or setting alerts for market movements. This can free up time for research, strategy refinement, or personal activities.

Time Management Apps: Use apps designed to help manage your schedule, set reminders, and track how you spend your time. These tools can be invaluable in identifying time sinks and optimizing your daily routine.

Integrating Rest and Rejuvenation

Scheduled Breaks: Integrate short breaks throughout your trading day to prevent fatigue and maintain mental clarity. Longer breaks or days off are crucial for deep rest and rejuvenation.

Vacations: Plan regular vacations or time away from trading to fully recharge. These periods can provide fresh perspectives and renewed energy, enhancing your trading performance upon return.

Reflect and Adjust

Regular Review: Periodically assess how well your time management strategies are working. Are you achieving your trading goals without sacrificing personal time or well-being?

Be Flexible: Be prepared to adjust your approach in response to changes in your trading strategy, market conditions, or personal life. Flexibility is essential for effective time management in the dynamic world of trading.

Effective time management is not about packing as much as possible into every day but about ensuring that each activity, whether related to trading or personal life, is performed with intention and purpose. By setting clear priorities, establishing boundaries, and utilizing technology, traders can create a balanced lifestyle that supports both their professional aspirations and personal well-being. Remember, the goal is to make trading a part of your life, not the entirety of it.

Relaxation and downtime play a crucial role in the life of a cryptocurrency trader, acting as the counterbalance to the high-intensity world of market fluctuations and trading strategies. Just as a finely tuned instrument needs rest to maintain its timbre, a trader requires downtime to maintain peak performance. This section underscores the importance of incorporating relaxation and downtime into your routine, offering suggestions for activities and practices that not only help unwind and recharge but also enhance overall well-being and trading efficacy.

The Importance of Relaxation and Downtime

Mental Clarity: Regular relaxation helps clear the mind, improving decision-making and problem-solving abilities, crucial for successful trading.

Stress Reduction: Engaging in relaxing activities lowers stress levels, mitigating the risk of burnout and maintaining emotional equilibrium.

Enhanced Creativity: Downtime can foster creativity, allowing for the development of innovative trading strategies and new approaches to market analysis.

Activities for Unwinding and Recharging

Yoga and Meditation

Yoga: Combining physical postures, breathing exercises, and meditation, yoga is an effective way to relieve stress, improve flexibility, and enhance mental focus.

Meditation: Regular meditation practice can reduce stress, increase calmness and clarity, and promote happiness. Even short daily sessions can have significant benefits.

Nature and Outdoor Activities

Spending Time in Nature: Activities like hiking, gardening, or simply walking in a natural setting can reduce stress, improve mood, and enhance cognitive function.

Outdoor Sports: Engaging in outdoor sports such as cycling, running, or swimming offers the dual benefits of physical exercise and exposure to fresh air and natural surroundings.

Creative Hobbies

Artistic Pursuits: Painting, drawing, music, or writing can be therapeutic outlets for expressing creativity and relieving stress. These activities offer a break from the analytical focus of trading.

DIY Projects: Engaging in do-it-yourself projects around the home or garden can provide a sense of accomplishment and a productive diversion from trading.

Social Activities

Quality Time with Loved Ones: Spending quality time with family and friends can provide emotional support, laughter, and a reminder of what's truly important beyond trading.

Group Activities: Joining clubs or groups that align with your interests, such as a book club, sports team, or cooking class, can expand your social network and provide a fun and rewarding way to unwind.

Mindful Relaxation

Mindfulness Practices: Incorporating mindfulness into your relaxation routine, such as mindful walking or savoring a meal without distractions, can enhance the restorative effects of downtime.

Deep Breathing Exercises: Simple deep breathing techniques can quickly reduce stress levels, making them a handy tool for relaxation anytime, anywhere.

Integrating Relaxation into Your Routine

Schedule Downtime: Treat relaxation and downtime as non-negotiable elements of your schedule, similar to trading hours and meetings.

Balance Activities: Incorporate a mix of physical, creative, and social activities into your downtime to address different aspects of well-being.

Be Present: Whatever activity you choose, focus on being fully present and engaged, allowing yourself to truly relax and recharge.

Recognizing the importance of relaxation and downtime is essential for sustained success in cryptocurrency trading. By regularly disconnecting from the pressures of the market and engaging in rejuvenating activities, traders can maintain their mental, emotional, and physical health, ultimately enhancing their trading performance and overall quality of life.

Holistic health, encompassing physical well-being through exercise, nutrition, and sleep, forms the foundation upon which successful cryptocurrency trading rests. Much like a sturdy vessel capable of navigating stormy seas, a healthy body ensures that a trader can withstand the pressures and demands of the market with resilience and clarity. This section delves into the crucial components of physical health and elucidates how they collectively influence mental acuity and, by extension, trading performance.

Exercise: The Pillar of Physical and Mental Vigor

Regular Activity: Engaging in regular physical exercise, such as cardiovascular workouts, strength training, or flexibility exercises, not only bolsters physical health but also enhances mental sharpness and emotional stability. Exercise improves blood flow to the brain, fostering cognitive function, and releases endorphins, which mitigate stress and boost mood.

Routine Integration: Incorporate exercise into your daily routine, finding activities that you enjoy and can commit to long-term. Whether it's a morning jog, a midday yoga session, or an evening bike ride, the key is consistency and enjoyment.

Nutrition: The Fuel for Body and Mind

Balanced Diet: A diet rich in vegetables, fruits, whole grains, lean proteins, and healthy fats provides the nutrients necessary for optimal body and brain function. Like high-quality fuel in an engine, the right foods can enhance energy levels, improve focus, and stabilize mood swings.

Hydration: Adequate water intake is crucial for maintaining energy levels and cognitive function. Dehydration can lead to fatigue, impaired memory, and difficulty concentrating.

Mindful Eating: Pay attention to your body's hunger and fullness signals, and avoid mindless eating, especially under stress. Consider the timing of meals to ensure you have the energy needed for peak trading hours.

Sleep: The Keystone of Health and Performance

Quality and Quantity: Aim for 7-9 hours of quality sleep per night to support physical repair, memory consolidation, and emotional regulation. Poor sleep can impair judgment, increase impulsivity, and reduce the ability to manage stress.

Sleep Hygiene: Establish a consistent sleep schedule and create a bedtime routine that promotes relaxation, such as reading or meditation. Ensure your sleeping environment is conducive to rest, considering factors like comfort, light, and temperature.

The Interconnectedness of Physical Health and Trading Performance

The direct link between physical health and trading efficacy cannot be overstated. Physical well-being influences mental clarity, emotional resilience, and energy levels, all of which are critical for making informed decisions, maintaining discipline, and executing strategies effectively in the fast-paced trading environment.

Stress Management: Regular physical activity and proper nutrition are powerful tools for managing stress, a constant companion in the trading world. They equip traders to face challenges with a level head and a calm demeanor.

Decision-Making: A well-rested mind, nourished by quality sleep and proper diet, is better equipped for the complex analytical tasks required in trading, from evaluating market conditions to executing trades.

Resilience: Holistic health practices build resilience, enabling traders to navigate the ups and downs of the market without succumbing to burnout or emotional extremes.

Emphasizing holistic health underscores the fact that trading is not merely a cerebral endeavor but a comprehensive lifestyle choice. By prioritizing physical health through exercise, nutrition, and sleep, traders can enhance their mental clarity, emotional balance, and overall trading performance, setting a course for long-term success and well-being in the high-stakes world of cryptocurrency trading.

Afterword

As we draw this guide to a close, it's crucial to recognize that the essence of cryptocurrency trading—and indeed, any form of trading—lies not in blindly following a set path but in carving out a journey that is uniquely yours. The world of cryptocurrency is vast and varied, offering a multitude of strategies, approaches, and philosophies. Success in this dynamic landscape is not a one-size-fits-all proposition. Each trader must navigate the market in a way that resonates with their personal goals, values, and lifestyle. This section of the Afterword emphasizes the importance of embracing your unique path in the world of cryptocurrency trading.

The Uniqueness of Every Trader's Journey

Your journey in cryptocurrency trading is as unique as your fingerprint. It is shaped by your individual goals, risk tolerance, time availability, and personal interests. Some may thrive on the adrenaline-fueled world of day trading, while others may find their niche in long-term strategic investments or delve into the specifics of a particular blockchain technology.

Discovering What Works for You

Personal Goals: Begin with clarity on your personal and financial goals. Are you trading for immediate income, long-term wealth building, or perhaps as a means to engage deeply with the blockchain technology space? Your goals will guide your strategy and how you measure success.

Risk Tolerance: Understanding and accepting your risk tolerance is key to defining your trading style. It influences your decision-making process, from the assets you choose to how much you're willing to invest and potentially lose in pursuit of gain.

Lifestyle Compatibility: Your trading approach should align with your lifestyle. Consider how much time you can dedicate to market research, trading, and staying updated on cryptocurrency news. A strategy that demands more time than you can commit is unsustainable.

Embracing the Learning Process

The journey to becoming a proficient cryptocurrency trader is a continuous learning process. Embrace the ups and downs as part of your growth, knowing that each challenge faced and obstacle overcome adds to your expertise and resilience.

Experimentation: Don't be afraid to experiment with different strategies within the bounds of your risk tolerance. This exploration is vital in discovering what truly works for you.

Reflective Practice: Regularly reflect on your trading experiences. What successes have you celebrated? What losses have you learned from? This reflective practice ensures your trading strategy remains aligned with your evolving goals and market conditions.

Staying True to Your Path

In the noise and fervor of the cryptocurrency market, it's easy to be swayed by the latest trends or the success stories of others. While learning from the community is invaluable, it's essential to remain true to your principles and the path you've charted for yourself.

Confidence in Your Strategy: Once you've found a strategy that aligns with your goals, risk tolerance, and lifestyle, have confidence in it. Market trends will come and go, but a well-thought-out strategy is your compass.

Adaptation and Growth: Stay open to adaptation. The cryptocurrency market is ever-evolving, and so too should be your approach. Adaptation is a sign of growth, not an admission of failure.

Your trading journey is deeply personal and uniquely yours. By embracing this journey, with all its individual quirks and contours, you position yourself not just for success in the markets but for a fulfilling experience that complements your life. Remember, in the world of cryptocurrency trading, the most successful path is the one that's authentically yours.

As you journey through the dynamic and often unpredictable world of cryptocurrency trading, embracing resilience in the face of adversity becomes a cornerstone of not just survival, but thriving. The path of a trader is inherently marked by peaks and valleys; it is the resilience cultivated during these times that defines and refines your journey. This segment aims to embolden you, reminding you that setbacks and challenges are integral to the landscape of trading, serving not as mere obstacles but as fertile ground for growth, learning, and eventual triumph.

Understanding the Nature of Trading

Trading, by its very essence, involves a degree of uncertainty and volatility. It's important to recognize that no strategy, no matter how meticulously crafted, can guarantee success on every trade. Markets fluctuate, trends reverse, and unforeseen events occur. This variability is not a flaw in the system but a feature of the financial markets, offering both risk and opportunity.

Embracing Setbacks as Learning Opportunities

Reframing Failure: Begin by reframing how you view setbacks. Instead of seeing them as failures, view them as integral steps in your learning journey. Each setback provides valuable data points, revealing what doesn't work and hinting at adjustments needed for improvement.

Analytical Review: After a setback, conduct a thorough review of your decisions and actions. What assumptions did you make? Were there warning signs you overlooked? This analytical approach transforms emotional responses into rational strategies for future trades.

Building Emotional Resilience

Mindfulness Practices: Engage in mindfulness and meditation to strengthen your emotional resilience. These practices help maintain equanimity, allowing you to face setbacks with a clear mind and steady heart.

Support Networks: Lean on your support network of fellow traders, friends, and family. Sharing your experiences can lighten the emotional load and provide you with fresh perspectives and encouragement.

Staying Committed to Continuous Improvement

Growth Mindset: Cultivate a growth mindset, viewing each trading day as an opportunity to learn and enhance your skills. Embrace the idea that mastery is a journey, not a destination.

Adaptation and Flexibility: Stay adaptable, willing to adjust your strategies in response to new information and market dynamics. The ability to pivot is a hallmark of a resilient trader.

Finding Strength in Adversity

Resilience as a Resource: Recognize that resilience itself is a resource that deepens with each challenge faced. Your capacity to bounce back becomes stronger with experience, enhancing your overall trading acumen.

Celebrating Small Victories: Acknowledge and celebrate your progress, no matter how small. These moments of acknowledgment fuel your journey, reminding you of your capabilities and potential.

Navigating the inevitable ups and downs of trading with resilience turns potential stumbling blocks into stepping stones. Remember, the journey of trading is as much about personal growth as it is about financial gain. The adversities you face are not just obstacles but opportunities to develop the grit, wisdom, and expertise that distinguish successful traders. In embracing this journey, with all its inherent challenges, you pave the way for not only professional achievement but also personal fulfillment and resilience that extends far beyond the markets.

Patience is a virtue, especially true in the high-stakes, rapidly changing world of cryptocurrency trading. In an arena where fortunes can seemingly be made or lost in the blink of an eye, the power of patience cannot be overstated. It's a quality that not only informs the execution of trading strategies with discipline and foresight but also underpins the broader arc of a trader's career development. This part of our closing wisdom emphasizes the critical role patience plays in nurturing sustainable success, encouraging traders to allow themselves the necessary time to learn, grow, and gradually achieve their goals.

Patience in Strategy Execution

Strategic Discipline: Patience empowers traders to stick to their strategies, even when immediate temptations beckon. It's the patience to wait for the right trade that meets all your criteria, rather than jumping at what seems like the next big opportunity.

Market Timing: Understanding that markets move in cycles and that opportunities will present themselves again is crucial. Patience means not chasing the market but waiting for it to align with your strategy, reducing the risk of impulsive decisions that can lead to losses.

Patience in Career Development

Learning Curve: Every trader's journey is replete with learning and adaptation. Patience is vital as you acquire new knowledge, skills, and experience. Mastery doesn't happen overnight, and giving yourself the grace to progress through stages of learning is essential.

Building Experience: With time, you'll encounter various market conditions, from bull runs to bear markets, each offering unique lessons. Patience allows you to accumulate a wealth of experiences, contributing to your depth as a trader.

Overcoming the Urge for Immediate Results

Long-term Perspective: Cultivate a long-term perspective, focusing on consistent growth over instant gains. The most successful traders are those who see beyond the immediate horizon, understanding that true wealth is built over time.

Embracing the Process: Learn to embrace the process of trading, finding satisfaction in the daily discipline, analysis, and decision-making. This mindset shifts the focus from outcomes to the quality of your trading practice.

Strategies to Cultivate Patience

Set Realistic Expectations: Understand the realistic timelines for achieving trading mastery and financial goals. Setting attainable milestones can help manage expectations and reinforce patience.

Mindfulness and Stress Management: Practices such as meditation, yoga, and regular physical exercise can help manage the stress that often fuels impatience, keeping you centered and focused.

Reflective Practice: Regularly reflect on your trading journey, acknowledging the progress you've made. This reflection can be a source of motivation and a reminder of the value of patience.

Patience is more than just waiting; it's an active, strategic choice that influences every aspect of trading and career development. It's the patience to develop a robust trading plan, the discipline to stick to it, and the wisdom to see beyond immediate outcomes. By cultivating patience, traders not only enhance their chances of success in the markets but also embark on a journey of personal growth and fulfillment. As you move forward, remember that patience is the companion of wisdom, guiding you to make considered decisions and to view your trading journey as a marathon, not a sprint.

Continual self-reflection is a critical practice for any trader seeking not just to survive but to thrive in the fluctuating world of cryptocurrency trading. It's akin to periodically checking your compass on a long journey, ensuring you're still heading in the direction you intended. This habit of introspection and evaluation allows traders to remain true to their personal values and objectives, adapting their strategies in response to both their successes and setbacks. In this final piece of parting wisdom, we underscore the significance of regular self-reflection in fostering a trading practice that is not only profitable but also personally fulfilling and aligned with your broader life goals.

The Importance of Self-Reflection

Personal Growth: Self-reflection facilitates personal growth by encouraging a deeper understanding of your trading decisions, emotional responses, and the outcomes of your actions. It helps you recognize patterns in your behavior that may be beneficial or detrimental to your trading performance.

Strategy Refinement: By regularly assessing what strategies work and which don't, you can refine your approach, eliminating ineffective practices and reinforcing those that yield positive results.

Alignment with Values and Goals: Continuous self-reflection ensures that your trading decisions and strategies remain aligned with your personal values and long-term objectives. It helps prevent drifting into trading patterns that may not serve your best interests or align with your risk tolerance.

Practices for Effective Self-Reflection

Keep a Trading Journal

Document Trades and Emotions: Maintain a detailed trading journal that records not just the trades you make but also the emotions and thought processes behind those decisions. This record becomes a valuable resource for reflection, allowing you to analyze your trading behavior over time.

Set Regular Review Sessions

Schedule Reflection Time: Set aside regular intervals—be it daily, weekly, or monthly—for reviewing your trading journal and overall performance. Use this time to ask yourself critical questions about the successes, failures, and unexpected outcomes you've encountered.

Ask the Hard Questions

Evaluate Decisions: Ask yourself whether your trading decisions were driven by analysis and strategy or if they were influenced by emotions or external pressures.

Assess Alignment: Consider whether your trading activities and outcomes are moving you closer to your personal and financial goals.

Identify Learning Opportunities: Look for lessons in both your successful and unsuccessful trades. What can you learn from each experience, and how can this knowledge inform your future trading decisions?

Embrace Change and Adaptation

Be Open to Adjustments: Based on your reflections, be willing to make changes to your trading strategy, risk management practices, or even your goals. Adaptation is a sign of growth and responsiveness to the market's and your personal evolution.

Seek Feedback

Engage with Peers: Sometimes, self-reflection can be enhanced by external perspectives. Engage with a trusted mentor or trading peers to discuss your reflections and gain insights from their experiences.

Continual self-reflection is an indispensable tool in the trader's arsenal, enabling not just the fine-tuning of strategies but also the deepening of self-awareness and personal integrity. It fosters a trading practice that is not only successful in financial terms but also enriching and sustainable, aligned with who you are and what you value. As you move forward on your trading journey, let self-reflection be your guiding light, illuminating the path to both professional mastery and personal fulfillment.

Embarking on a journey of continuous learning is essential for staying competitive and informed in the rapidly evolving world of cryptocurrency trading and blockchain technology. The landscape is rich with resources, but navigating this wealth of information can be overwhelming. To aid in this endeavor, below is a curated list of reputable online platforms offering a diverse array of courses, webinars, and workshops. These resources are designed to enhance your knowledge, whether you're a novice seeking foundational understanding or a seasoned trader aiming to refine your skills and stay ahead of market trends.

Coursera

Offerings: Coursera provides a wide range of courses on cryptocurrency and blockchain technology from leading universities and companies. Topics range from Bitcoin and cryptocurrency technologies to more advanced courses on blockchain development and financial technology.

Features: Courses often include video lectures, interactive quizzes, and peer-reviewed assignments, offering a comprehensive learning experience.

Udemy

Offerings: Udemy boasts an extensive library of courses on cryptocurrency trading strategies, technical analysis, blockchain development, and cryptocurrency fundamentals.

Features: With courses frequently updated to reflect the latest trends and practices, Udemy allows learners to study at their own pace, with lifetime access to purchased courses.

edX

Offerings: edX offers courses in partnership with renowned institutions, covering topics such as Bitcoin and cryptocurrencies, blockchain technology, and the legal implications of blockchain innovations.

Features: edX provides learners with the opportunity to earn verified certificates, adding value and recognition to their educational endeavors.

CryptoCompare

Offerings: CryptoCompare features a range of beginner-friendly guides and articles on various aspects of cryptocurrencies, including how to trade, invest, and understand different coins and tokens.

Features: It's a great starting point for those new to crypto, providing foundational knowledge in an easily digestible format.

CoinDesk

Offerings: Known for its news coverage, CoinDesk also offers educational content that helps readers understand the complexities of blockchain technology and the cryptocurrency market.

Features: Its learning section is suitable for traders and enthusiasts looking to deepen their understanding of the industry's latest developments.

Cointelegraph

Offerings: Cointelegraph University offers a selection of free courses designed to educate about cryptocurrencies, blockchain, and how the technology is changing the face of finance.

Features: These courses are aimed at both beginners and those looking to expand their knowledge, with insights from industry experts.

Blockchain Council

Offerings: This platform offers comprehensive training and certifications in various blockchain and cryptocurrency domains, tailored for those looking to deepen their technical expertise.

Features: Courses are detailed and cover a wide range of topics, from blockchain basics to specific programming languages used in blockchain development.

Khan Academy

Offerings: Khan Academy provides free courses on money, banking, and financial markets, including a section on cryptocurrencies that covers the basics of Bitcoin and the concept of cryptocurrencies.

Features: Known for its educational approach, Khan Academy is ideal for beginners and those who prefer structured, academic-style learning.

Engaging with these platforms can significantly enhance your understanding and performance in cryptocurrency trading and blockchain technology. By dedicating time to continuous learning, you position yourself to make more informed decisions, adapt to market changes, and ultimately achieve your trading and investment goals. Remember, the field is always advancing, and staying informed is key to navigating its challenges and seizing its opportunities.

In the vast ocean of knowledge that encompasses cryptocurrency trading and blockchain technology, books and publications stand as lighthouses, guiding traders through both the technical intricacies and the psychological complexities of this dynamic field. The following curated selection of books and publications has been carefully chosen to enhance your understanding, strategy, and mindset as a cryptocurrency trader. Whether you're delving into the technical depths of blockchain or seeking to master the mental game of trading, these essential reads offer valuable insights and guidance.

Technical Aspects of Trading and Blockchain

"The Bitcoin Standard: The Decentralized Alternative to Central Banking" by Saifedean Ammous

A profound exploration of the economic properties that have allowed Bitcoin to emerge as a viable alternative to central banks, offering readers a thorough understanding of cryptocurrency's potential impact on the global financial system.

"Mastering Bitcoin: Unlocking Digital Cryptocurrencies" by Andreas M. Antonopoulos

This book provides a comprehensive guide to the revolutionary technology of Bitcoin and how it works under the hood. It's an essential read for anyone looking to truly understand the mechanics of Bitcoin and blockchain technology.

"Blockchain Basics: A Non-Technical Introduction in 25 Steps" by Daniel Drescher

Perfect for those new to blockchain, this book breaks down the concepts into easily digestible sections, making the technology accessible to readers without a technical background.

Psychological Components of Successful Trading

"Trading in the Zone: Master the Market with Confidence, Discipline, and a Winning Attitude" by Mark Douglas

A seminal work on the psychological aspects of trading, this book emphasizes the importance of attitude, discipline, and confidence in achieving trading success, offering strategies to overcome mental barriers.

"The Psychology of Trading: Tools and Techniques for Minding the Markets" by Brett N. Steenbarger

This book dives into the psychology behind trading, offering insights into how to improve performance through understanding and controlling psychological responses to market movements and trading pressures.

Comprehensive Guides on Cryptocurrency Trading

"Cryptoassets: The Innovative Investor's Guide to Bitcoin and Beyond" by Chris Burniske and Jack Tatar

Offering a blend of technical analysis and investment strategies, this book provides a detailed overview of the investment landscape of cryptoassets, making it a valuable resource for investors looking to diversify their portfolios.

"Digital Gold: Bitcoin and the Inside Story of the Misfits and Millionaires Trying to Reinvent Money" by Nathaniel Popper

Through the tales of Bitcoin's early adopters and innovators, this book offers a fascinating look at the history and development of cryptocurrency, providing context and insights into its future potential.

Periodicals and Online Publications

CoinDesk and Cointelegraph: These online platforms are not just news sources but also feature analytical articles, op-eds, and research reports that provide deeper insights into market trends, technological advancements, and regulatory changes in the crypto space.

The Block: Known for its in-depth research and analysis, The Block offers comprehensive reports and articles on various aspects of cryptocurrency markets, blockchain technology, and the digital asset space.

Each of these books and publications offers a unique lens through which to view the multifaceted world of cryptocurrency trading and blockchain technology. By engaging with these resources, traders can equip themselves with the knowledge and insights necessary to navigate the markets with confidence, strategic acumen, and a balanced mindset.

Navigating the dynamic and sometimes tumultuous waters of cryptocurrency trading requires not just individual skill and knowledge but also the collective wisdom and support of a community. Online communities, forums, and social media groups serve as invaluable resources, offering spaces for discussion, advice, and camaraderie among fellow traders. Here, you'll find a curated list of platforms where you can engage with others who share your interest in cryptocurrency trading, blockchain technology, and financial markets. Whether you're seeking advice, looking to share insights, or simply wanting to connect with like-minded individuals, these communities can enhance your trading journey.

Reddit

r/CryptoCurrency: One of the largest communities dedicated to general discussions about cryptocurrency. It's a place for sharing news, strategies, and experiences.

r/Bitcoin: Focused specifically on Bitcoin, this subreddit is a hub for discussions about Bitcoin news, investment strategies, and technical developments.

r/Ethereum: Dedicated to Ethereum, this community discusses everything from the latest project developments to investment strategies and market analysis.

Discord

The Crypto Gateway: Offers discussions on a wide range of topics in crypto trading, including technical analysis, market trends, and upcoming ICOs.

Crypto Cartel Original: Known for its active trading community, Crypto Cartel Original provides a platform for real-time trading discussions, market analysis, and sharing of strategies.

Telegram

ICO Speaks: This group is centered around ICOs, providing news, reviews, and discussions about upcoming and ongoing ICO projects.

Trading Crypto Coach®: Focuses on trading signals, strategies, and advice for both novice and experienced traders looking to navigate the crypto markets.

BitcoinTalk

An early forum created by Bitcoin creator Satoshi Nakamoto, BitcoinTalk remains a vital source of information and discussion for cryptocurrency enthusiasts. It features sections on technical discussions, mining, and altcoins.

Twitter

Twitter hosts a vibrant crypto community, with many traders, analysts, and influencers sharing insights and updates. Following hashtags like #crypto, #bitcoin, and #blockchain can lead you to valuable content and discussions.

CryptoCompare

Offers a forum where users can discuss cryptocurrencies, wallet options, mining solutions, and the latest news within the community.

Stack Exchange

Bitcoin Stack Exchange: A question-and-answer site for Bitcoin crypto-currency enthusiasts. It's a great place for technical questions and answers about Bitcoin and blockchain technology.

Engaging with these online communities and forums can significantly enrich your understanding of cryptocurrency trading and blockchain technology. By participating actively, you can gain insights from diverse perspectives, stay updated on the latest trends and developments, and find encouragement and support from fellow traders. Remember, the strength of the community lies in the collective knowledge and shared experiences of its members. As you dive into these communities, approach them with openness, respect, and a willingness to contribute, fostering a positive environment for learning and growth.

Mentorship and networking are indispensable pillars for anyone looking to deepen their expertise and expand their horizons in the realm of cryptocurrency trading. These avenues offer a unique blend of personal guidance, shared experiences, and professional connections that can significantly accelerate your learning curve and open doors to new opportunities. This section aims to encourage traders to actively seek out mentorship opportunities and engage in networking events, both virtual and in-person, to foster meaningful relationships with experienced traders and industry professionals.

Seeking Mentorship

Identify Potential Mentors: Look for mentors who not only have the trading expertise and success you aspire to but also share your values and approach to trading. Mentors can be found through online communities, social media platforms, or trading forums.

Engage with Respect and Value: When reaching out to a potential mentor, be clear about what you're seeking from the relationship and what you can bring to it. Remember, mentorship is a two-way street that requires mutual respect and value exchange.

Leverage Formal Programs: Some trading platforms and educational institutions offer formal mentorship programs. These programs can provide structured support and learning opportunities from seasoned traders.

Networking Opportunities

Attend Industry Conferences and Meetups: Conferences, seminars, and meetups provide excellent opportunities to meet other traders and professionals in the blockchain and cryptocurrency sectors. These events can offer insights into market trends, investment strategies, and emerging technologies.

Participate in Virtual Webinars and Workshops: With the rise of virtual events, geographical barriers no longer hinder networking. Participate in webinars, online workshops, and virtual meetups to connect with a global community of traders and experts.

Join Trading Clubs and Societies: Local or online trading clubs and societies can be valuable resources for meeting peers with similar interests. These groups often host regular meetings, guest speaker events, and trading competitions.

Benefits of Mentorship and Networking

Accelerated Learning: Direct guidance from a mentor and insights gained from networking can fast-track your learning process, helping you to avoid common pitfalls and refine your trading strategy more quickly.

Support and Encouragement: Trading can be a solitary endeavor. Having a mentor and a network provides emotional support, encouragement, and a sense of community that can be motivating during challenging times.

Diverse Perspectives and Opportunities: Engaging with a broad network of individuals offers diverse perspectives that can enhance your understanding and approach to trading. Additionally, networking can open doors to opportunities such as partnerships, investments, and even career advancements.

Tips for Effective Mentorship and Networking

Be Proactive and Engaged: Take the initiative to reach out, ask questions, and participate in discussions. The more engaged you are, the more you'll gain from mentorship and networking opportunities.

Offer Value in Return: Consider how you can offer value to your mentors and networking contacts. This could be through sharing your own insights, providing support to others, or contributing to the community in meaningful ways.

Maintain Professionalism: Whether interacting online or in person, maintain professionalism in all communications and engagements. Building a positive reputation in the trading community can have long-lasting benefits.

Mentorship and networking are not just about building professional connections; they're about joining a community of like-minded individuals who can inspire, challenge, and support you on your trading journey. By actively seeking out these opportunities, you open yourself to a wealth of knowledge, experiences, and connections that can enrich your trading career and personal growth.

In the demanding world of cryptocurrency trading, where the stakes are high and the market never sleeps, prioritizing well-being is not just beneficial—it's essential. The intersection of physical and mental health plays a pivotal role in a trader's ability to maintain focus, make sound decisions, and withstand the inherent stresses of the market. To support traders in nurturing their well-being, here is a collection of resources focusing on physical health, mental resilience, and overall well-being. These resources include mindfulness apps, exercise programs tailored for busy schedules, and nutritional guides, all designed to integrate seamlessly into the trader's lifestyle.

Mindfulness and Meditation Apps

Headspace: Offers guided meditations, mindfulness practices, and sleep exercises designed to reduce stress and improve focus. It's suitable for beginners and seasoned practitioners alike.

Calm: Features a wide array of mindfulness and meditation resources, including sleep stories, music, and guided sessions to help users reduce anxiety and improve sleep quality.

Insight Timer: Boasts the largest free library of meditation and mindfulness content, with thousands of guided meditations, music tracks, and talks by mindfulness experts.

Exercise Programs for Busy Schedules

7 Minute Workout: Based on high-intensity circuit training, this app is perfect for traders with limited time, offering quick workouts that can be done anywhere, without any equipment.

Yoga With Adriene: An online yoga platform offering free, high-quality yoga videos for all levels, including yoga practices for stress relief, focus, and overall fitness.

Fitness Blender: Provides a vast selection of free workout videos, ranging from strength training and cardio to Pilates and yoga, catering to different fitness levels and time constraints.

Nutritional Guides and Resources

MyFitnessPal: A comprehensive tool for tracking diet and exercise, helping users monitor their calorie intake and maintain a balanced diet tailored to their fitness goals.

Precision Nutrition: Offers extensive guides and articles on healthy eating, including meal planning, recipes, and nutritional strategies for stress management and energy improvement.

The Mediterranean Dish: Features healthy, easy-to-prepare recipes based on the Mediterranean diet, known for its benefits on heart health and longevity.

Holistic Well-being Resources

The Wellbeing Thesis: An online resource offering comprehensive support on well-being, including managing stress, improving sleep, and enhancing work-life balance, tailored for those in high-pressure environments.

The Mindful Trader: Focuses on the mental and emotional aspects of trading, offering strategies to manage stress, cultivate mindfulness, and maintain a positive mindset amidst the ups and downs of the market.

NutritionFacts.org: A non-commercial, science-based source for the latest in nutrition research, offering videos, articles, and blogs on how diet can affect overall health and well-being.

Integrating these well-being resources into your daily routine can significantly impact your trading performance and personal satisfaction. By dedicating time to mindfulness, physical activity, and nutritional health, traders can build a foundation of resilience that not only supports their trading endeavors but also enriches their overall quality of life. Remember, a healthy trader is a more effective trader, and prioritizing well-being is an investment that yields dividends in all areas of life.

www.ingramcontent.com/pod-product-compliance
Lightning Source LLC
Chambersburg PA
CBHW062102220526
45471CB00010B/3571